VOID

Library of
Davidson College

The Law of Contracts

by
Margaret C. Jasper

Oceana's Legal Almanac Series:
Law for the Layperson

1995
Oceana Publications, Inc.
Dobbs Ferry, N.Y.

Jasper, Margaret C. The Law of Contracts

ISBN: 0-379-11192-6

Copyright 1995 by Oceana Publications, Inc.

All rights reserved. No part of this publication may be reproduced or transmitted in any form or by any means, electronic or mechanical, including photocopy, recording, xerography, or any information storage and retrieval system, without permission in writing from the publisher.

Manufactured in the United States of America on acid- free paper.

ISSN: 1075-7376

ABOUT THE AUTHOR

MARGARET C. JASPER is an attorney engaged in the general practice of law in Armonk, New York, concentrating in the areas of domestic relations, employment law, entertainment law, and civil litigation. Ms. Jasper holds a Juris Doctor degree from Pace University School of Law, White Plains, New York, is a member of the New York and Connecticut bars, and is certified to practice before the United States District Courts for the Southern and Eastern Districts of New York. She has been appointed to the panel of arbitrators of the American Arbitration Assocation and the law guardian panel for the Family Court of the State of New York, and is a New York State licensed real estate broker and member of the Westchester County Board of Realtors, operating as Jasper Real Estate, Armonk, New York.

TABLE OF CONTENTS

INTRODUCTION................................... ix

CHAPTER 1: THE SOURCE OF CONTRACT LAW
In General 1
Common Law 1
Statutory Law 1

CHAPTER 2: CONTRACT FORMATION
In General 3
The Offer.. 3
Commitment 3
Communication................................... 4
Definite Terms 5
Acceptance of the Offer 6
Acceptance Under a Unilateral Contract............ 6
Acceptance Under a Bilateral Contract............. 6
Consideration 8
First Element: Bargained For Exchange 8
The "Past Act" Rule 8
Exceptions to the "Past Act" Rule.................. 9
Second Element: Detriment to the Promisor 10
The "Pre-Existing Duty" Rule..................... 10
Exceptions to the "Pre-Existing Duty" Rule 10
Third Element: A Binding Promise 11
Adequacy of Consideration....................... 11
The Agreement 11
The Parol Evidence Rule......................... 12
Plain Language Laws 14

CHAPTER 3: DEFENSES TO FORMATION OF A VALID CONTRACT
In General 15
Formation Defect 15
Statute of Frauds................................ 16
In General 16
Types of Protected Contracts 16
Kinds of Tangible Evidence Necessary for Enforceability... 17
Incapacity 18
Illegality 19
Misrepresentation/Fraud......................... 20

Duress 21
Unconscionability 21
Mistake 22

CHAPTER 4: CONTRACT CONDITIONS

In General 25
Express Conditions 25
Duty to Perform 25
Constructive Conditions 26
Timing of Performance of the Condition 27
Excusing the Condition 27
Satisfaction of the Condition 29

CHAPTER 5: CONTRACT DUTIES

Discharging Duties 31
Satisfying Duties 34

CHAPTER 6: TERMINATION OF A CONTRACT OFFER

Termination of an Offer Prior to Acceptance 35
Termination by Revocation 35
Termination by Rejection 35
Termination by Operation of Law 36
Irrevocable Offers 37
Counter-Offers 38
Counter-Offers in Non-UCC Contracts 39
Counter-Offers Governed by the UCC 39

CHAPTER 7: BREACH OF CONTRACT AND REMEDIES

In General 41
Remedies 41
Damages 41
Breach by Person Contracted to Perform Services . 41
Breach by Person who has Contracted to Have Services
    Performed 42
Miscellaneous Damages 43
Mitigation of Damages 43
Liquidated Damages 43
Damages Under Quasi-Contracts 44
Specific Performance 44
Arbitration 45

CHAPTER 8: CLASSIFICATION OF CONTRACTS

Divisible and Indivisible Contracts 47
Executed and Executory Contracts 47
Express and Implied-in-Fact Contracts 47
Gratuitous and Onerous Contracts 48
Unilateral and Bilateral Contracts 49
Void and Voidable Contracts 49
Option Contracts 50
Guaranty 50

CHAPTER 9: NON-PARTY RIGHTS

In General 53
Third Party Beneficiaries 53
Intended vs. Incidental Beneficiaries 53
Creditor vs. Donee Beneficiaries 54
Enforceability 54
Assignments 55
Restrictions on Assignability 56
Method of Assignment 56
Enforceability 57
Delegations 58
Enforceability 58
Novation 59

CHAPTER 10: THE UNIFORM COMMERCIAL CODE

In General 61
Offer 62
In General 62
Total Output and Requirements Contracts 62
Firm Offer 63
Acceptance 64
Counter-Offers 65
Modifications 65
Casualty to Identified Goods 65
Identified Goods 65
Risk of Loss 66
Performance 67
Breach of Contract 67
Seller's "Status Quo" Remedies 67
Seller's "Right of Resale" Remedies 68
Buyer's "Status Quo" Remedies 68
Buyer's Procedures to Exercise Remedies 69
The Statute of Frauds 69

In General 69
Exceptions 70
The Parol Evidence Rule 70
In General 70
Exceptions 71
Unconscionability 71

APPENDICES

APPENDIX 1 - ANALYSIS OF A SIMPLE CONTRACT 73

APPENDIX 2 - CAPACITY TO CONTRACT ACCORDING TO STATE MINIMUM AGE 79

APPENDIX 3 - DIRECTORY OF STATE CONSUMER PROTECTION AGENCIES 81

APPENDIX 4 - SAMPLE BREACH OF CONTRACT NOTIFICATION 87

APPENDIX 5 - SAMPLE STANDARD CONTRACT ARBITRATION CLAUSE 89

APPENDIX 6 - SAMPLE AGREEMENT TO SUBMIT A DISPUTE TO ARBITRATION 91

APPENDIX 7 - SAMPLE REAL ESTATE PURCHASE OPTION CONTRACT 93

APPENDIX 8 - SAMPLE GUARANTY 95

APPENDIX 9 - SAMPLE ASSIGNMENT OF CONTRACT .. 97

APPENDIX 10 - UNIFORM COMMERCIAL CODE: STATE ADOPTION OF ARTICLE 9 RELATING TO SALES AND SEURED TRANSACTIONS 99

GLOSSARY 101

BIBLIOGRAPHY 113

INTRODUCTION

There is a common admonition concerning the importance of "reading the fine print" before "signing on the dotted line." Of course, the "dotted line" refers to the place where one signs a contract of some type.

Most people seek professional guidance when they contemplate signing a complex agreement, such as when they are purchasing a home, or forming a partnership. However, people frequently enter into equally binding agreements, such as credit card agreements and apartment leases, without first consulting a lawyer. All too often, such common agreements are handed to the consumer without any expectation that the fine print will actually be read. Most boilerplate language contains so much legalese that the average layperson would have to consult a legal dictionary to understand the terms. Often, it not until a dispute arises, that the individual attempts to scrutinize the agreement.

For example, when your credit card payment is a few days late, and you discover that a $20 late fee has been assessed, you may be surprised to discover that paragraph 26 on page 2 of the application you signed gave the company the absolute right to assess the penalty.

This legal almanac explores the law of contracts in an attempt to make this complex area of law more understandable to the layperson. The almanac discusses the necessary requirements to form a valid, enforceable contract, and the remedies available should there be a breach of the contract. The almanac explains common contract clauses and analyzes a simple contract.

The Appendix provides samples of common contractual clauses, applicable statutes and other pertinent information and data. The Glossary contains definitions of many of the terms used throughout the almanac.

CHAPTER 1: THE SOURCE OF CONTRACT LAW

In General

Contract law is primarily derived from judicial decisions, known as the common law, and from statutory law, such as the Uniform Commercial Code. Secondary authority supporting the evolution of contract law comes from sources which influence judicial decision making, such as restatements of the law, treatises, and law reviews.

Common Law

Common law involves the application of precedent, i.e., the adherence to past judicial decisions in resolving similar disputes. This process provides some degree of predictability in the outcome of a dispute, and also serves to prevent judges from rendering decisions based on their own biases.

In order for the judge to be bound by a prior decision, the precedent case must have been decided in the same court and jurisdiction, or in a higher court. A judge may decide to avoid applying the precedent by distinguishing the facts in the precedent case from the facts of the case to be decided. If the judge is unable to distinguish the case, he or she may overrule the precedent. This is a drastic measure and is typically only done when the precedent case is unjust or outmoded.

Statutory Law

The Legislature has ultimate law making power, providing the laws it enacts are constitutional. The Legislature has the power to change common law. Therefore, all courts are bound by statutory law. Each state has devised a set of laws which governs contracts. Most of those statutes are adaptations of the Uniform Commercial Code (UCC), which is more fully discussed in Chapter 10. Because state laws may vary, the reader is advised to consult the law of the state which governs the particular contract.

CHAPTER 2:   CONTRACT FORMATION

In General

A contract is an agreement between two or more persons which creates an obligation to do, or refrain from doing, a particular thing. In order to form a valid contract, there must be (1) an offer; (2) acceptance of the offer; (3) consideration; and (4) a mutual agreement by the parties as to the subject matter of the contract, i.e. a "meeting of the minds." An analysis of a simple contract is set forth in the Appendix.

The Offer

An offer is a proposal to do something, or pay an amount, which is usually accompanied by an expected acceptance, a counter-offer, or a return promise or act. The offer permits the offeree the power to accept the offer thus making the offeror's promise a contractual obligation.

For example, A tells B that B may purchase A's watch for fifty dollars. This is an offer by A to sell A's watch to B for a sum of money. If B agrees to pay A the sum of money, B is deemed to have accepted the offer. This confers a contractual obligation on A to turn the watch over to B upon the payment of fifty dollars.

As set forth below, there are three basic requirements of a valid offer.

1. Commitment

There must be clear commitment, or intention, by the offeror, to make the offer. The existence of commitment is judged objectively. For example, one must consider whether a reasonable person, hearing the words spoken, under the circumstances in which they were spoken, would believe that the speaker intended to enter into a contract.

One must first examine the spoken words. For example, if A states that he or she "promises" to perform a particular act, a valid offer may have been made thus establishing a contract. However, if A states that he or she will "consider" performing a particular act, it is less likely that this language constituted a valid offer.

One must also examine the circumstances surrounding the offer. For example, if the words are spoken irrationally, such as in anger or fear, it is less likely that there was a bona fide offer.

There are other factors which may help to establish whether or not a valid offer has been made, such as the prior course of dealing between the parties, and the custom of the industry in which the parties operate.

2. Communication

There must be communication of the offer by the offeror to the identified offeree, and the offeree must have actual knowledge of the offer in order to accept it.

For example, A tells B's brother, C, that A would like to offer his car for sale to B for $1000. C states that he's sure B would want to buy A's car. In the meantime, A buys another car, relying on the income he expects to receive from the sale of his old car to B. A delivers his car to B, however, C did not tell B about the offer. B refuses to buy A's car. A sues B. A will lose because B had no actual knowledge of the offer. Thus, no valid contract was formed between A and B.

In addition, the offer is considered personal to the identified offeree and cannot be transferred. For example, continuing with the foregoing fact pattern, C brings $1000 to A, expecting that A will sell him the car. A refuses. C sues A in an attempt to force A to sell him his car. C loses because the offer was meant for B, not C. Thus, no valid contract was formed between A and C.

An exception to the communication requirement exists in the context of a public offer, such as an offer of reward. Obviously, there cannot be identification of the offeree until someone (a) knows that the offer exists and (b) performs the requested act.

For example, A places signs around his neighborhood offering a reward for the return of his lost dog. A cannot yet know who is going to find and return the dog, therefore, A cannot identify the offeree. The identified offeree must first read the sign to gain actual knowledge of the offer, then find and return the dog, to complete performance. At that point, A is obliged to pay the reward money to B.

Nevertheless, if someone were to perform without actual knowledge of the offer, there is no contract because one cannot accept an offer one knows nothing about. For example, if B found and returned A's dog without ever reading the sign, A would not be obligated to pay B the reward money.

3. Definite Terms

An offer must contain definite and certain terms. It is no longer necessary that an offer define all material terms in order to be valid. However, the offer must at least define, with certainty, the subject matter of the contract, so as to show that the parties had a meeting of the minds" on the most basic aspect of the contract. The court may furnish all other material terms of a disputed contract with reasonable terms.

For example, a contract for the sale of real property must at least provide the sale price, and the a description of the property to be sold. An employment contract must at least state the term of the employment. However, even when the term is not clearly stated, the employment contract may be considered an offer for employment at will, thus enabling the employee to leave the position for any reason whatsoever without repercussion.

This rule assumes that the offer is silent on all other terms except the subject matter. If the offer attempts to address any other material term, that term must be made with certainty to be enforceable. Nevertheless, if the subject matter is provided, the contract will be enforceable even though some of the material terms may not be enforceable.

For example, A tells B that he will sell B his car, and that he will "consider" fixing the brakes first. In that case, B can force A to sell the car because the sale is the subject matter of the contract. B cannot force A to fix the brakes because that term was not stated with sufficient certainty to be enforceable.

An estimate is not an offer. For example, A asks B, a painter, to provide an estimate for painting A's home. B's estimate is $2,000.

After B finishes painting A's home, he hands A a bill for $2,200. A is liable to B for the full amount of $2,200. The estimate was not an offer and the law allows for some variation.

Acceptance of the Offer

There must be acceptance of the offer, and the offer must not have been terminated prior to the acceptance. The contract type dictates the manner in which acceptance must be made.

1. Acceptance Under a Unilateral Contract

A unilateral contract exists when the offeror has clearly warned the offeree that the only way to accept the offer is to completely perform the requested act. Complete performance constitutes acceptance of the offer, at which time the contract is formed.

Many states also require that the offeror receive notice of completion of performance if the offer states that there must be notice. In addition, most states require notice to the offeror if completion of performance would not otherwise come to the offeror's attention.

2. Acceptance Under a Bilateral Contract

A bilateral contract proposes acceptance of an offer by a promise which is made expressly or by conduct.

(a) Express Acceptance - For there to be express acceptance of an offer, there must be both commitment and communication. Commitment is judged by the same objective test used in determining whether a valid offer has been made.

For example, one must consider whether a reasonable person, hearing the words spoken, under the circumstances in which they were spoken, would believe that the speaker intended to accept the offer. Again, one must look at the spoken words; examine the circumstances surrounding the acceptance; and look at the prior course of dealing between the parties and the custom of the industry in which the parties operate.

Communication of acceptance of an offer must be made. If the offer explicitly states the manner in which acceptance must be made, e.g., by certified mail, then the only way one can accept that offer is by certified mail. However, if the offer does not state the manner in which acceptance must be communicated, then acceptance may be validly made in the same manner the offer was received. For example, if the offer was made by telephone, then acceptance may also be made by telephone.

Thus, acceptance of an offer should be made in a manner as efficient and dependable as the manner in which the offer was made. For example, if the offer was made by regular mail, then acceptance may be made by regular mail. A faxed acceptance may also suffice, since it is as efficient and dependable as regular mail. However, acceptance by telephone would probably not be valid because it is not made in writing as was the offer.

It should be noted that acceptance will generally be effective upon dispatch, even if the offeror is not aware that the acceptance has been sent, providing that it is properly addressed with postage prepaid. An exception exists where the offer states that acceptance is not effective until actually received by the offeror.

(b) Acceptance By Conduct - Acceptance by conduct exists if there has been commencement of performance instead of a promise to perform. For example, A promises to pay B $500 to repair A's roof. A expects B to accept by making a return promise to repair the roof. Instead, B begins working on the roof.

Many states consider that a valid contract has been formed if one accepts the benefit of unsolicited goods. For example, if you mistakenly received a subscription for a magazine and then read the magazine, this may be considered an implied promise to pay for the magazine. Some states, however, would consider unsolicited goods an unconditional gift.

Consideration

Consideration is the inducement to enter into a contract. Consideration may involve some right, interest, profit, or benefit which accrues to one party, or some forbearance, detriment, loss or responsibility undertaken by the other party. Simply stated, the consideration is what each party bargains for in the agreement.

For example, A offers to sell A's watch to B for the sum of $100. B accepts and pays A $100. B gets the watch. A bargained so that A could receive money and B bargained so that B could receive the watch.

Consideration is an essential component of an enforceable contract. There must be at least one consideration supported promise from each party to the contract for consideration to exist. One must examine the individual promises made by both the offeror and offeree when trying to determine whether consideration is present To determine whether consideration exists for each individual promise, the following three elements must be present:

First Element: A Bargained For Exchange

One must ask if the promise induces current performance from the promisee, i.e. does the promise ask for something in return?

For example, A offers to sell his television to B for $500. Thus, A is asking B for a current exchange of $500 for A's television.

If the promise asks for nothing in return, e.g., if A simply promised to give B his television for free, there is no consideration supported promise and thus no enforceable contract. The television would merely be considered a gift. This is so even if the promise asks for some immaterial thing in return. For example, if A told B he could have his television as long as B arranged to pick it up, although A is asking for something in return, i.e., that A retrieve the television, consideration would not likely be found.

The "Past Act" Rule

An important element in determining the presence of consideration is that the promise must induce "current" performance from the promisee. This means that past acts are not a basis for consideration, and promises based on past acts are not enforceable.

For example, B rescues A from drowning in the ocean. A is so grateful that he promises to give B $10,000 for rescuing him. This promise is not enforceable because the act of rescue is a past act and cannot be the basis for consideration.

Exceptions to the "Past Act" Rule

There are some exceptions to the "past act" rule, as follows:

(a) In many states, the promise will be enforceable if the past act was performed as follows: (i) If the act was performed at the request of the promisor; and (ii) If there was an expectation of payment on the part of the promisee.

(b) In a minority of states, a promise for past acts will be enforceable provided that (i) There is a writing which sets forth the past act for which the promise was made; and (ii) The past act would have been good consideration if it had been made contemporaneously with the promise.

(c) There is also a public policy exception to the past act rule which exists to encourage people to pay their debts even if the debt is barred by a technical defense, such as the statute of limitations.

Thus, if a promise is made to pay a debt after the statute of limitations has expired, the writing will revive the debt and it will again be enforceable provided that (i) The promise is made in a writing which recognizes the debt; and (ii) The debt cannot be increased and the debtor can only be liable for the amount stated.

For example, A loaned B $500. B paid a total of $100 to A. The statute of limitations expired and legally, B would not be liable to A for the balance of $400. Nevertheless, if B sends A another $100 payment with a note stating that B knew he still owed A $400 and planned to pay the debt in full, the debt would revive and B would again be liable for it.

Second Element: Detriment to the Promisor

One must determine whether the promise offers detriment to the promisor. If the promisor will be placed at a legal disadvantage such that he or she is offering to do something that they would not otherwise be legally required to do; or if the promisor has foregone something he or she had a legal right to do, the promise may be enforceable.

In a minority of states, if detriment to the promisor cannot be found, they will look to see whether there was any benefit to the promisee. Consideration may be found if the promisee detrimentally relied on the offer.

For example, A knew that B was going to buy a television set for which B was to receive a reduced price. A told B to forego the sale because A had a perfectly good television he never used, and A was willing to give it to B for free. In the meantime, A's primary television broke and A reneged on the promise to give B the other television. The television on sale was no longer available. The court may find a binding contract because B detrimentally relied on A's promise.

The "Pre-Existing Duty" Rule

Similar to the "past act" rule, detriment that was already legally owed will generally not be good consideration because there was already a pre-existing legal duty.

Exceptions to the "Pre-Existing Duty" Rule

There are certain exceptions to the pre-existing duty" rule, as follows:

> (a) If unforeseen circumstances arise that are severe enough to prevent the promisor from performing, thus rescinding the duty to perform, then a new promise to perform for new consideration will be enforceable.

> (b) If there is a bona fide dispute over what the duties are, then new promises made to resolve the dispute are enforceable.

Third Element: A Binding Promise

One must determine whether the promise is binding and not merely illusory. A promise is illusory if performance is at the unrestricted discretion of the promisor. In that case, one party has an alternative which, in reality, is an empty promise because nothing of value is actually exchanged.

For example, A promises B that he will sell B his car in exchange for B's promise to either pay A $100 or not pay A any money at all. In this case, if B elects the latter option -- not to pay

A any money at all -- there is no exchange and the agreement lacks consideration.

Adequacy of Consideration

The court generally does not concern itself with the fairness or adequacy of the consideration. However, on occasion, if the consideration appears patently unfair or grossly inadequate, the court may rule that the contract is unenforceable due to unconscionability. This would be particularly likely where the parties were in unequal bargaining positions or when one party is found to have taken unfair advantage of the other. To avoid such an outcome, the parties to the contract should recite facts which adequately explain why the provision in question is, in fact, fair.

Many agreements contain the following clause: "For $1.00 and other good and valuable consideration, receipt of which is hereby acknowledged, the parties agree as follows..." This clause is routinely used as a boilerplate recitation of consideration, whether or not the $1.00 is actually paid. It is also used in agreements where the parties wish to keep the actual sale price confident. Although commonly used, one should be cautioned that the $1.00 consideration clause" may raise questions as to the inequality of the exchange. It is safer to specify the mutual promises with particularity.

The Agreement - A Meeting of the Minds

There must be an agreement by both parties as to the subject matter and terms of the contract. There must be mutual assent, i.e. a "meeting of the minds." Nevertheless, a reasonable manifestation of assent may suffice.

For example, A is serious about entering into a contract with B, however, B is joking. A has no reason to believe that B was joking, therefore, a binding contract may still be found. However, if both A and B agree that they were only joking, there is no contract.

The Parol Evidence Rule

The Parol Evidence Rule seeks to preserve the integrity of written agreements by refusing to permit contracting parties to attempt to alter their written contract through the use of contemporaneous parol, i.e. oral declarations. The purpose of the Parol Evidence Rule is to provide the parties to the contract some certainty as to their rights and obligations under the contract.

For example, A offers to sell his 1967 Mustang Convertible to B for the sum of $3,000. B inspects the car and tells A how much he likes the expensive CD/cassette stereo system B installed in the car. The stereo system plays a big part in B's decision to accept A's offer to purchase the car.

A provides B with an agreement for the sale of the car. The agreement simply states that A agrees to sell his 1967 Mustang Convertible to B for the sum of $3,000 in cash. The agreement also contains a small paragraph which provides that the contract is final and binding upon the parties, contains the entire understanding of the parties and any modification must be in writing. B signs the agreement and goes to the bank to withdraw the money for the car.

In the meantime, A removes the stereo system, which A plans to use in another car, and replaces it with the standard AM-FM radio originally installed in the car. B returns and pays A the contract price of $3,000. A hands B the keys and B drives away. As B heads down the road, he notices that the stereo system has been replaced. He returns to A and demands that A either give him the stereo system or his money back. A tells B that he is under no obligation to give B the stereo system, and refers B to the terms of their written agreement.

B sues A. B will likely lose. Pursuant to the Parol Evidence Rule, B will not be able to introduce the conversation between A and B concerning the stereo system.

Thus, if the parties have a final written agreement, then no prior oral or written negotiations, or contemporaneous oral negotiations, may be introduced into evidence, to vary or contradict the terms of the final written agreement. All previous oral agreements merge in the writing and the terms of the writing control. The only exception would be a showing of fraud, duress, mistake, undue influence, incapacity or illegality, in which case parol evidence would be admissible. In addition, if an agreement is ambiguous on a certain point, parol evidence is admissible to explain the ambiguity.

To determine whether an agreement is, in fact, final, the following factors must be considered:

1. The language of the agreement states that it is final, e.g., there is a merger or integration clause in the agreement. A sample merger clause is set forth in the Appendix.

2. Where the agreement is silent as to finality, the court must examine both the agreement and the parol evidence and decide according to the standard of whether a reasonable person similarly situated would have put the parol evidence into the agreement. If the answer is yes, then the parol evidence is not admissible and the contract is determined to be final. If the answer is no, then the parol evidence is admissible and the contract is considered to be only partially integrated. In that case, a collateral oral agreement is admissible and, if established, enforceable.

Thus, all relevant evidence is admissible to determine the issue of finality, including the parol evidence.

Parol evidence only covers prior or contemporaneous evidence. Any evidence which occurred subsequent to the agreement, even if it varies or contradicts the terms of the agreement, is admissible. State and local laws vary, however, some states have enacted statutes which provide that a contract cannot be changed except by a subsequent written agreement.

Plain Language Laws

Most people have been confronted with a contractual document that contained numerous paragraphs of fine print legalese. Such language is common in standard form contracts, such as leases and consumer credit agreements. This creates a dilemma for the layperson because such transactions are not commonly those for which expending legal fees are desirable. Therefore, most people make an attempt at deciphering the contract language without legal guidance, and end up signing without a complete understanding of the agreement.

Largely due to the consumer activist movement, various state legislatures have attempted to address this problem by enacting "Plain Language" laws which require that certain consumer contracts be written so that the average layperson can understand them. The two general categories of plain language laws which have been enacted are the general/subjective laws and the specific/objective laws.

The general/subjective plain language laws generally require that the drafters ensure the language contained in the contract is sufficiently clear, containing common usage words, so that the layperson can understand what they are signing. In addition, the layout of the contract is generally required to be clearly set forth, with its various sections appropriately labeled and subdivided.

The specific/objective plain language laws set forth an elaborate scoring system which must be adhered to in order to be deemed acceptable. A common objective test used in plain language statutes is known as the Flesch test of reading ease. The Flesch test computes a score based on the measurement of the number of syllables in each word and the number of words in each sentence. The theory behind this objective test is that shorter words in shorter sentences are more easily understood. In addition to the Flesch test, there are certain specific requirements concerning the size of the type and layout of the contract.

CHAPTER 3: DEFENSES TO THE FORMATION OF A VALID CONTRACT

In General

A contract is generally enforceable if all of the conditions for forming a valid contract have been met, unless there exists a defense to enforcing the contract, such as:

1. Formation Defects

2. Statute of Frauds

3. Incapacity

4. Illegality

5. Misrepresentation/Fraud

6. Duress

7. Unconscionability

8. Mistake

Each of the above defenses is explained more fully below:

Formation Defects

As previously set forth in Chapter 2, in order to have formed a valid contract, the following requirements must be present:

    (a)   An offer;

    (b)   Acceptance of the offer;

    (c)   Mutuality, i.e., a meeting of the minds; and

    (d)   Consideration

If one of the above elements is missing, an enforceable contract will not likely be found.

Statute of Frauds

In General

The statute of frauds, also known as the statute of frauds and perjuries, is derived from a 1677 English statute which was modified and adopted by almost all of the United States. It prohibits the initiation of lawsuits based on certain categories of contracts, unless the particular contract is substantiated by a writing which was signed by the party to be charged, or the party's authorized agent.

The purpose of the statute of frauds was to combat fraud and perjury in the making of contracts. It is designed to protect certain contracts which are deemed to be so valuable, or so easily imagined, that the party's word alone is not sufficient to enforce the contract. The statute of frauds does not make a contract void, however, it does make the contract either voidable or enforceable dependent upon the tangible evidence which is submitted.

Types of Protected Contracts

Following are some of the types of contracts which may be protected under the Statute of Frauds depending on the applicable state laws:

1. Contract Involving Insurance - For example, the provisions relating to assigning the contract or changing the beneficiary.

2. Contract for Commission or Finders Fee - For example, involving the sale of a business or real estate.

3. Contract Where Marriage is the Consideration - For example, prenuptial agreements or separation agreements.

4. Contract to Answer for the Debt of Another - In the majority of states, such a contract is protected as long as the promise is not made for the benefit of the promisor. For example, A wants to borrow money for a car but needs B to cosign for a loan. B agrees to cosign but only if A allows B to drive the car whenever he wants. This contract would not be protected by the statute of frauds be-

DEFENSES TO THE FORMATION OF A VALID CONTRACT

cause the main purpose of B's promise to cosign was to benefit B, the promisor.

5. Contract Involving Real Property Interests - A contract involving real property interests is viewed as unique and valuable and is, therefore, protected by the statute of frauds. However, the subject matter of the contract must be the real property, such as in the context of a sale; mortgage or lease, and the term must exceed one year.

6. Contract that Cannot be Completed Within One Year After Formation - To determine whether the contract is protected by the statute of frauds, one must first examine whether there is any conceivable way that the contract could be fully completed in one year.

7. Contract for the Sale of Goods Over $500 - Such a contract is protected provided that it is (a) in writing or there has been either full or partial performance; or (b) for specially manufactured goods; or (c) a merchant confirmed an oral offer for goods in a writing and the offeror fails to object.

Kinds of Tangible Evidence Necessary For Enforceability

1. Any kind of a signed, written statement which adequately specifies the essential terms of the contract is sufficient to substantiate that a contract existed. Specifically, the writing should contain the following:

   (a) Identification of the parties to the contract;

   (b) A description of the subject matter of the contract;

   (c) A description of the consideration for the contract; and

   (d) The signature of the party to be charged.

It should be noted that a contract can be written on practically anything, e.g. a paper napkin, and still be an enforceable contract.

2. Partial or Full Performance Under the Contract

If there is partial or full performance under the contract by one of the parties, this may be tangible evidence of the existence of a contract, as follows:

(a) If there has been partial performance, the contract will be enforceable to the extent of the performance.

(b) If there has been full performance, the contract will be fully enforceable.

Incapacity

Incapacity is generally defined as the lack of legal ability to act due to diminished or absent physical or intellectual power; or a natural or legal disqualification. A contract is unenforceable against -- and voidable by -- a party who lacked the capacity to enter into the contract. Nevertheless, if the party thereafter acquires capacity, they can affirm the contract either (a) expressly; or (b) by accepting the benefits of the contract. In either case, the contract is thus made enforceable.

There are three basic categories of incapacity:

(a) Infancy - An infant is deemed to be any person under the age of legal competence. As set forth in the table found in the Appendix, most states have set the age of legal competence at eighteen. A minor generally can only enter into voidable contracts, i.e., ones which the minor -- or their legal guardian -- can cancel unilaterally.

In some cases, if the minor had purposely misrepresented his or her age, the minor may not be permitted to avoid the contract. Thus, it is prudent to include a clause in the contract stating that the parties are of sufficient age to enter into the contract. The clause can thereafter be used to prove misrepresentation should the minor attempt to avoid the contract.

(b) Mental Incompetency - A person who does not have the ability to appreciate the nature of the contract is deemed mentally incapable of entering into a contract. If the person has been adjudicated incompetent by a court of law, a contract with that person would be void. If the person has not been adjudicated incompetent, but is still mentally incapable of appreciating the nature of the contract, a contract with that person is voidable and unenforceable. Nevertheless, the contract can be affirmed during any moments of lucidity by the incompetent.

(c) Intoxication - A person who is intoxicated -- under the influence of either alcohol or drugs -- at the time he or she signed the contract, in all likelihood cannot appreciate the nature of the contract. However, in order to find the contract unenforceable, you must also show that the other party knew, or should have known, that the party was intoxicated, and he or she then tried to take advantage of the intoxicated person's condition by presenting the contract at that time.

Therefore, if the intoxicated party appears to the other party to be in full control of his mental faculties, the contract may still be enforceable against the intoxicated person.

Illegality

Illegality is defined as that which is contrary to the principles of law. There are two basic types of illegality relating to contracts:

(a) Illegal Contract - An illegal contract is one in which the subject matter of the contract is illegal, such as a contract to commit murder. An illegal contract is void and unenforceable by any party.

(b) Illegal Purpose - An illegal purpose exists where the subject matter of the contract is legal, but the purpose of the contract is illegal, such as the rental of an airplane for the purpose of smuggling drugs. A contract which has an illegal purpose is voidable against the party who knew of the illegal purpose.

Certain contracts may have an element of illegality in them yet still be enforceable. For example, if one obtains a loan from a finance company, and the loan company charges interest at a rate which is higher than the legal interest rate, a court may still uphold the contract, but will reform it by lowering the illegal interest rate so as to uphold the bargain and enforce the contract.

Misrepresentation/Fraud

Misrepresentation is defined as any manifestation by words or other conduct, by one person to another, that under the circumstances amounts to an assertion that is not in accordance with the facts. A misrepresentation which justifies the rescission of a contract is a false statement of a substantive fact which is material to the proper understanding of the matter in hand, and which was made with the intent to deceive or mislead.

The misrepresentation defense, also known as the fraud defense, involves two distinctions:

(a) Fraud in the Execution of the Contract - Fraud in the execution of a contract, also known as "fraud in factum," occurs when a party has been deceived into entering into the contract, not being aware that it was a contract he or she signed. Such a contract is void and unenforceable.

(b) Fraud in the Inducement - Fraud in the inducement to enter into a contract occurs when the party is aware that he or she is signing a contract, but is deceived as to the subject matter of the contract. Such a contract is voidable by the party who was defrauded. Nevertheless, if the defrauded party chooses to enforce the contract, he or she may do so.

Nondisclosure is also a type of fraud which occurs when a person fails to disclose a fact known to him, when he knows that disclosure would correct a misunderstanding of the other party as to a basic assumption of the contract. Non-disclosure of a fact may be taken as an assertion that the fact does not exist. The court would likely find that there has been bad faith dealing on the non-disclosing party.

For example, the seller of a house has the duty to reveal defects which are latent and dangerous of which only the seller is aware. The defect must be material, significant, or propose a latent dangerous condition, and go to the heart of the deal. If there is a termite condition in the house, this would be a serious latent defect in that the termite condition could destroy the structure of the home.

DEFENSES TO THE FORMATION OF A VALID CONTRACT

Duress

Duress is defined as a condition where one is induced by the wrongful act or threat of another, to enter into a contract under circumstances which would deprive that person of his or her exercise of free will. A contract induced by duress is unenforceable. It is either void or voidable.

The duress defense involves two basic distinctions:

(a) Personal Duress - personal duress occurs when a person is forced to enter into a contract. For example, a gun is placed to their head and they are forced to sign on the dotted line." Such a contract is always voidable by the party who was placed under duress.

(b) Economic Duress - Economic duress occurs when one party seeks to take advantage of the other party's unfortunate financial situation. Nevertheless, economic duress cannot be used as a defense to the enforceability of a contract unless the party taking advantage of the situation has also caused the negative economic condition.

Unconscionability

The defense of unconscionability applies to all contracts. Unconscionability refers to an absence of meaningful choice on the part of one of the contracting parties, together with contract terms which are unreasonably favorable to the other contracting party. This is often found where one of the parties to the contract has the stronger bargaining power, and uses it to pressure the other party to agree to unfair terms.

Nevertheless, because the court is reluctant to pass judgment on contracts which were voluntarily and openly entered into, it would likely uphold such a contract absent a showing of true unconscionability.

To be deemed unconscionable, the contract must have been unfair and oppressive to one of the parties under the terms existing at the time the contract was formed.

For example, A enters into a contract with B to lease a piece of property for a term of 10 years, with an option to buy the property for the sum of $25,000 at the end of the term of the lease. During the term, new construction and development of the area causes the property values to skyrocket. At the end of the term, A attempts to exercise the option and pay B the sum of $25,000. B claims that the contract is unconscionable -- and thus unenforceable -- because the property is presently appraised at $325,000.

The court may find the contract enforceable because although the deal may appear unfair under the present economic conditions, the terms of the contract were fair at the time the parties entered into the contract.

Standardized agreements often contain potentially unconscionable provisions which are set forth in fine print or located inconspicuously within the document. Such provisions are apt to be found unconscionable. To avoid a finding of unconscionability, provisions which appear potentially unconscionable should be set forth in plain language and set apart from the rest of the contract, such as in bold or highlighted print.

Most jurisdictions have enacted Consumer Protection Acts to protect consumers from unfair or deceptive acts or practices, such as the unconscionable, illegal and unenforceable provisions often hidden within standardized consumer credit contracts. Consumer Protection Acts confer liability upon the violators of the provisions of the Acts. A Directory of Consumer Protection Agencies is set forth in the Appendix.

Mistake

Mistake exists when a person does something, or fails to do something, due to some erroneous conviction of law or fact. There are three distinct mistake defenses:

> (a) Mutual Mistake - A mutual mistake occurs when the parties to the contract agree upon a subject matter that does not exist. Such a contract is void.

For example, an antique dealer sells what he believes to be a genuine Louis XIV chair to a collector. The collector thereafter discovers that the chair is, in fact, a replica. This is a mutual mistake by both parties to the contract, therefore, the contract is void.

(b) Unilateral Mistake - A unilateral mistake occurs when one party to the contract makes a mistake as to a term of the contract. Such a contract is fully enforceable unless the other party knew or should have known that the mistake was being made.

(c) Ambiguous Material Term - If the contract contains an ambiguous material term, i.e., a term which can be interpreted in more than one way, the contract is unenforceable unless both parties agree that they intended the same meaning for the ambiguous term. However, if one of the parties to the contract was aware of the ambiguity, and the other party was unaware of the ambiguity, the contract may be enforced according to the understanding of the "innocent" party.

CHAPTER 4: CONTRACT CONDITIONS

In General

A condition is a future and uncertain event which must occur, unless it is excused, before performance under a contract becomes due.

For example, A's car is stolen. He reports the theft to his insurance company. Insurance Company is obligated under the terms of A's insurance policy to pay A for his loss. However, a condition of payment is that A provide Insurance Company with proof that the car was stolen, e.g. a police report. Thus, the condition which must occur before the Insurance Company performs, i.e., pays A, is the submission by A of a police report.

Express Conditions

Express conditions are those conditions set forth in the terms of the contract. They modify the promise contained in the contract. They act to either support the duty or prevent performance of the duty.

Duty to Perform

Enforcement of the duty depends, in part, on the control each party has in meeting the condition, as shown in the following scenarios.

For example, A agrees to sell his house to B if it rains on the following Saturday and B agrees to buy A's house if it rains on the following Saturday. The condition is that it rain on Saturday. Neither A nor B have any control over whether it rains on Saturday, thus this is a true condition of the contract.

If A agrees to sell his house to B for $50,000 if B obtains financing, and B agrees to buy A's house if B can obtain financing, there exists a condition--that B obtain financing. However, since B has control over this condition in that he must apply for financing and follow through with the process, there also exists a covenant for B to use good faith in bringing about the event which will satisfy the condition. If B does not pursue financing in good faith, then A may sue B for performance, i.e. to buy the house.

If A agrees to paint B's house, and B agrees to pay A $1,000 if B is satisfied that A has done a good paint job, there exists both a condition and a covenant of good faith on both parties. The conditions are that A provide a good paint job and that B make payment for the paint job. Thus, both parties have control in that they must make a good faith effort to have the event occur.

Constructive Conditions

Constructive conditions occur as follows:

1. When one party's performance under the contract precedes the other party's performance, the first party's performance is a constructive condition to the second. For example, A agrees to sell his car to B and to deliver the car on January 1st. B agrees to pay for the car on January 15. There are no apparent conditions, however, a construction condition will hold up because B's duty never matures until A performs, that is, A's delivery of the car on to B on January 1st is a constructive condition precedent to B's duty to pay A.

2. When one party's performance under the contract takes longer than the other party's performance, the longer performance is a constructive condition to the former. For example, A agrees to pay $1,000 to B and B agrees to paint A's house. A's duty to pay is subject to the constructive condition precedent of B's painting the house.

3. When there is simultaneous performance under the contract, both performances are constructively conditioned concurrently on each other. For example, A agrees to sell his car to B for $500 and B agrees to pay A $500 for the car. They both agree that the transfer will take place on January 1st. This constitutes simultaneous performance of conditions which are to occur concurrently.

CONTRACT CONDITIONS

Timing of Performance of the Condition

The conditions contained in a contract may be required to be performed at various points in time, as follows:

1. Condition Precedent - A condition precedent is one which must be performed before the agreement becomes effective. A condition precedent requires the occurrence of some event or the performance of some act before the contract is binding on the parties and must be completed before the duty under the contract matures.

2. Condition Concurrent - A condition concurrent exists when the parties to the contract are subject to mutual conditions precedent.

3. Condition Subsequent - A condition subsequent is a provision giving one party the right to divest himself of liability and obligation to perform further if the other party fails to meet the condition. The condition subsequent must occur after the duty. The condition then acts to discharge the duty.

Excusing the Condition

Conditions must be either excused or satisfied in order for the duty to occur. The party whose performance is conditioned must perform regardless in the following situations:

1. Failure to Cooperate or Prevention of the Occurrence of the Condition - The party whose performance is conditioned must perform regardless of whether there is failure to cooperate, or if there is prevention of the occurrence of the condition. If A agrees to sell his house to B for $100,000 on the condition that B gets financing, then B must cooperate in obtaining financing. If B does not cooperate in obtaining financing, or otherwise prevents the financing from occurring, then B must still perform and buy the house anyway.

2. Anticipatory Repudiation - Anticipatory repudiation occurs when the party whose performance is conditioned repudiates the contract.

For example, A agrees to buy B's house for $100,000 on the condition that it rains on the following Saturday. If A then repudiates the contract by saying he will not buy B's house even if it rains on Saturday, A will be required to perform, i.e. buy B's house, whether or not it rains on Saturday.

When a party repudiates the contract, the breach may be accelerated and the condition excused, as follows:

a) If repudiation occurs before the other party has performed, the repudiation accelerates the breach and excuses the condition.

b) If the repudiation occurs after the other party has performed, you cannot accelerate the breach.

c) If a party is unsure whether a breach is coming, he or she may demand adequate assurance that performance will occur. Adequate assurance must be in writing and received within a reasonable amount of time. Under the UCC, a reasonable time is deemed to be 30 days. If the potentially breaching party fails to respond, then there is a repudiation and all the effects of a repudiation come into play as described above.

3. Voluntary Disablement - Voluntary disablement is anticipatory repudiation by conduct. In this case, the repudiating party does something that prevents performance. This operates to excuse all the conditions for performance and accelerate the breach if it occurs before the other party's performance.

For example, if A agrees to sell her car to B for $500, but before B pays, A sets fire to the car thus preventing performance, the breach of the agreement is accelerated and all of the conditions for performance are thus excused.

4. Estoppel - Estoppel occurs when the party whose performance is conditioned, prior to the time the event is to occur, states that they don't care whether the event occurs and they will perform anyway. If the other party changes his or her position as a result of this statement, then estoppel occurs an the condition is excused.

For example, A says he will buy B's house for $100,000 if A obtains financing. A then says that he will buy B's house whether or not he is able to obtain financing. B relies on this statement and turns down other potential buyers for his house. In this case, A has the duty to perform and buy the house and the condition that A obtain financing is excused.

5. Waiver - Waiver occurs when the party whose performance is conditioned on an event that did not occur, thereafter states that he or she will perform anyway. Using the foregoing fact patter, if A applies for financing, but is rejected, and A thereafter states to B that he will nevertheless buy the house, A has a duty to buy the house even though a was unable to obtain financing.

The difference between estoppel and waiver is that estoppel occurs before the condition was to take place and waiver occurs after the condition was to take place.

Satisfaction of Conditions

If a condition has not been excused, as set forth above, then it must be satisfied in order for the duty to occur. Satisfaction can occur as follows:

1. Complete Satisfaction - Complete satisfaction occurs when all of the conditions are met. Complete satisfaction is required for all express conditions.

For example, A agrees to buy B's house for $100,000 if it rains on the following Saturday. It must rain on Saturday in order for A to be obligated to buy B's house.

2. Substantial Satisfaction - Substantial satisfaction occurs when all conditions other than express conditions require substantial satisfaction.

For example, if A agrees to paint B's house for $1,000 and A substantially completes painting B's house, the duty to pay matures.

3. Divisibility Doctrine - the divisibility doctrine states that if there are divisible portions of a contract, you don't have to wait until the entire performance is completed to have the duty arise.

For example, if a contract requires A to paint 10 house located in a subdivision, and A substantially paints the first house, there is a duty to pay A for painting the first house even before he starts painting the second house.

CHAPTER 5: CONTRACT DUTIES

Discharging Duties

There are eight ways a duty contained in a contract can be discharged, as follows:

1. Modification - Modification is the term used when the parties are changing the duties under the original contract. If a modification is enforceable, then the original duties are discharged and new duties arise based on the modification. For example:

Original Duty - A agrees to buy a ring from B on January 1st for $500.

Modification - A and B agree that A will instead buy the ring from B on February 1st for $250.

Outcome - The duty to deliver changed from January 1st to February 1st and the duty to pay $500 changed from $500 to $250.

2. Mutual Rescission/Cancellation/Release - If there is mutual rescission, cancellation or release of the duties contained in the contract, this eliminates the requirement of performance of those duties.

For example, A agrees to buy B's house for $100,000 and B's household furniture for $10,000. A thereafter says he only wants to buy the house and B agrees. This eliminates both the duty to deliver and the duty to pay for the household furniture.

3. Accord and Satisfaction - Accord and satisfaction occurs when the parties to the original contract resolve a dispute existing in the contract and make a new agreement to satisfy the dispute.

For example, A agrees to buy B's house, including its contents, for $125,000. A believes he is agreeing to buy everything in the house, including all of the household furniture. B believes it means he is only selling the house and the fixtures. In order to resolve the dispute, the parties make a new written agreement which states that A will buy the house for $100,000 and B will remove the household furniture.

The accord, i.e., the new agreement, does not in itself eliminate the duties under the old contract. It is the satisfaction -- the payment of the $100,000 and the removal of the household furniture -- that eliminates the duties under the old contract. If there is no satisfaction, i.e., performance of the accord, then a lawsuit can be brought to enforce the terms of the original contract.

4. Novation - A novation involves the substitution of a new party and new performance in place of the old party and old performance.

For example, A agrees to sell B his ring for $500. B thereafter changes his mind and tells C to buy A's ring instead. A, B and C agree. B's obligation to buy the ring is discharged and C is now obligated to purchase the ring.

A novation is not an assignment or delegation because neither A nor B are unilaterally introducing the third party, C, into the contract. In a novation, all three parties agree. Because all parties agreed, B can never be sued nor sue on the original contract.

5. Impossibility - Impossibility means that the contract cannot be performed at all by anyone because of an event that has occurred, in which case all duties are discharged and nobody can be sued. Impossibility occurs as follows:

(a) If the subject matter of the contract has been destroyed before performance, e.g., on a contract of sale for a house, if the house burns down, the duty to perform is discharged.

(b) In a contract for personal services, if the performer dies or is otherwise incapacitated, the duty to perform is discharged.

(c) In a supplier contract, if the sole source of the supply is destroyed, the duty to perform is discharged.

(d) If there is a supervening illegality wherein a law is passed that says the parties are no longer permitted to do the act which the contract required, the duty to perform is discharged.

Under the UCC, impossibility is termed "casualty to identified goods," and is more fully discussed in Chapter 10.

6. Impracticability - Impracticability occurs when a party can't perform at the time because of some unforeseen, severe and unassumed event that makes it unreasonable to perform as written in the contract. If the event which makes performance impracticable is temporary, the duties are merely suspended until the event ceases, at which time the duties to perform arise promptly. If the event which makes performance impracticable is permanent, then it is likened to impossibility and there is a discharge of duties.

For example, A agrees to install an inground pool in B's backyard on June 1st, which requires the workers to dig a large hole in the ground. However, it is raining on June 1st and the workers thus cannot perform. A thereafter refuses to perform because he is backed up with other jobs for the next 6 months. This constitutes a breach because A had the duty to perform promptly once the temporary condition -- the rain -- was resolved. However, had A's crew began the job and found that the backyard was solid rock preventing them from digging the necessary hole, this would constitute a permanent event and the duty to perform would be discharged.

7. Frustration - Frustration occurs when the purpose of the contract no longer exists. Therefore, if some unforeseen

event acts to cancel the purpose of the contract, and both parties knew of the purpose of the contract, then all duties are discharged.

For example, A agrees to pay B to babysit for A's children because A desires to work outside the home. However, A is unable to find suitable employment. Thus, the purpose of the agreement -- to provide care for A's children while A is not home -- no longer exists and B's duty to care for A's children and A's duty to pay B are discharged.

8. Failure to Excuse or Satisfy a Condition Subsequent - Chronologically, this occurs after the duty to perform occurs. The duty must be excused or satisfied. If the duty is not excused or satisfied, the duty is alive and must be performed or a breach occurs.

Satisfying Duties

Duties may be satisfied as follows:

1. Complete Performance - Complete performance is always required for any express term of a contract.

2. Substantial Performance - If there has been substantial performance, there must be payment.

3. Divisibility Doctrine - The divisibility doctrine states that, if there are divisible portions of a contract, you don't have to wait until the entire performance is completed to have the duty arise.

CHAPTER 6: TERMINATION OF A CONTRACT OFFER

Termination of an Offer Prior to Acceptance

In general, an offer is freely terminable prior to acceptance, and is accomplished by (1) revocation; (2) rejection; or (3) operation of law, as set forth below.

1. Termination by Revocation

Prior to acceptance, an offeror can revoke an offer either (a) expressly or (b) by conduct.

(a) Express Revocation

Express revocation is effective when the offeree receives it. Actual knowledge by the offeree of the offeror's revocation of the offer is not required. It is effective upon receipt whether or not the offeree has yet read it. A public offer may be revoked in the same manner as made. For example, a reward which was advertised in a newspaper can be revoked provided that the revocation is advertised in a comparable medium. Thus, a reward which was initially advertised on national television cannot be revoked by publishing the revocation in a local newspaper.

(b) Revocation by Conduct

An offer can be revoked by conduct if the offeror does something that would prevent performance of the contract and the offeree gains knowledge of that fact from a reliable source. For example, A tells B that he will sell B his car for $500. B tells A he will let him know if he wants to buy the car by the next day. In the meantime, A sells the car to C. B subsequently discovers that C bought the car. Nevertheless, the following day, B returns to A with a check for $500 and asks for the car. A tells B that the car has been sold. B sues. B will likely lose because he knew that A had already sold the car to C before he accepted A's offer.

2. Termination by Rejection

Prior to acceptance, an offeree can reject an offer either (a) expressly or (b) by conduct.

(a) Express Rejection

Express rejection occurs when the offeree refuses the offer or when the offeree communicates a counter-offer. An express rejection is effective when the offeror has received it. As with express revocation, actual knowledge by the offeror of the offeree's rejection of the offer is not required. It is effective upon receipt whether or not the offeror has read it.

(b) Rejection by Conduct

Rejection by conduct occurs when the offeree lets the offer lapse. For example, if the offeror states that the offer is open for 7 days and the offeree makes no effort to accept the offer within that 7 day period, the offer is deemed rejected by conduct. If the offer does not provide a time period within which it must be accepted, it will be deemed open for a reasonable period of time.

Once an offer has been rejected, it can never be revived, even if the offeree subsequently attempts to accept the offer. In that case, the offeree would be deemed to have made a new offer and would thus be acting as the offeror. Such is the case with a counter-offer, which is explained more fully later in this chapter.

For example, A offers B a contract of sale of A's car and states that the offer is open for 7 days. The following day, B declines the offer. Three days later, B attempts to accept the offer. A is not bound to sell the car to B because once B rejected the offer, it could not be revived. In effect, B's attempt to accept the offer may be deemed a counter-offer which gives A the right to accept or decline selling the car to B.

3. Termination by Operation of Law

An offer may be terminated by operation of law in the following three ways:

(a) Intervening Event - Something occurs before acceptance has taken place which makes it impossible to follow through with the offer.

For example, A offers to sell his car to B, however, before B can accept the offer, A's car is stolen.

(b) Supervening Illegality - The offer will be terminated if a law is passed which prevents the contract from being performed.

For example, A offers to sell B an antique pistol for $500. In the meantime, a law is passed prohibiting the private sale or transfer of all firearms, including antiques and collectibles, between individuals. A's offer is thus terminated because it would be illegal for A to now sell the gun to B.

(c) Death or Incapacity - The death or incapacity of either the offeror or offeree will terminate the offer.

For example, A offers to sell B her car for $500. B dies shortly thereafter. B's son, C, attempts to accept the offer. A refuses to sell her car to C and C sues. C will lose because the offer was meant for B. A is not obligated to extend the offer to anyone other than B.

Irrevocable Offers

There are certain offers which cannot be terminated and thus deemed irrevocable, as follows:

1. Merchant's Firm Offer - In many states, in connection with the sale of goods, if a merchant puts an offer in writing stating that it will be held open, that offer is irrevocable for the time stated in the writing, or for a reasonable amount of time if the writing is silent as to the time period. A reasonable amount of time is generally deemed to be no more than 3 months of time unless consideration has been paid to the merchant to extend the time period.

For example, on October 1st, a wholesaler faxes a written offer to a supermarket for the seasonal half-price sale of 500 turkeys @$2.00 per turkey for a total cost of $1,000. The offer states that it will be open until November 20th. On November 19th, the supermarket sends a fax to the wholesaler, accepting the offer. Nevertheless, the supermarket is billed for the full price of the turkeys of $2,000. The supermarket is only obligated to pay the wholesaler the sum of $1,000.

2. Option Contract - In many states, if consideration is received by the offeror to keep the offer open for an agreed period of time, the offer is irrevocable for that period of time and is the subject matter of the option contract. In addition, if the offeree detrimentally, reasonably and foreseeably relies on the offer, this may be deemed a substitute for the required consideration.

For example, on January 1st, A leases his house to B for $750 per month with an option to buy the house for $50,000 on or before July 1st. In the meantime, A discovers that the area will be redeveloped and property values will soar over the next 3-5 years. On June 1st, B exercises his option to buy A's house. A is obligated to sell the house to B for $50,000.

In another example, a general contractor bids on a construction project and, in doing so, receives bids from various subcontractors to determine what he will bid on the project. Those subcontractor bids are considered offers. When the general contractor submits the bid, he or she detrimentally, reasonably and foreseeably relies on the subcontractor bids. Therefore, the subcontractor bids are deemed to be option contracts and the subcontractors must keep the bids open for the agreed time.

3. Unilateral Contract Offers - In many states, offers to make unilateral contracts -- contracts in which the offeror warns the offeree that the only way the offeree can accept is by completing performance -- are irrevocable for a period of time.

Counter-Offers

A counter-offer is defined as an offer made by an offeree to an offeror relating to the same matter as the original offer, and proposing a substituted bargain differing from that proposed by the original offer.

The method of making counter-offers differs depending on whether or not the contract is governed by the UCC.

Counter-Offers in Non-UCC Contracts

The acceptance of an offer must mirror the offer or it will be deemed a counter-offer. If the acceptance adds anything new or different to the original offer, a counter-offer is created which requires an acceptance by the original offeror.

For example, A tells B that he will sell his car to B for $5,000. B tells A that he will buy A's car for $5,000 if A replaces all of the tires on the car. Since B added an additional term to the original offer, his acceptance is considered a counter-offer which requires acceptance by A.

Counter-Offers Governed by the UCC

The UCC sets forth various rules concerning counter-offers in connection with the sale of goods which are set forth in Chapter 10.

CHAPTER 7: BREACH OF CONTRACT AND REMEDIES

In General

A breach of contract occurs when one has an absolute duty to perform under a contract but fails to perform even though performance was not excused. A sample Notice of Breach of Contract is set forth in the Appendix.

Remedies

The remedies for breach of contract differ depending on whether or not the contract was governed by the UCC. Breach of contracts governed by the UCC is covered in Chapter 10. This chapter covers the remedies for breach of non-UCC contracts. The remedies for breach of contract are basically (1) money damages; and (2) specific performance, where feasible.

Money Damages

Damages are defined as the pecuniary compensation or indemnity which may be recovered in court by any person who has suffered loss, detriment, or injury, whether to his person, property or rights, through the unlawful act or omission or negligence of another.

In general, the measure of damages for a breach of contract is to put the non-breaching party in as good a position as if the breach had not occurred and performance had been completed.

Breach By Person Contracted to Perform Services

The damages for breach of a contract to perform services is for the promisee to get the benefit of the bargain. There are two basic measures of damages in this case: (1) The Cost of Completion Measure; and (2) The Diminution in Value Measure.

1. The Cost of Completion Measure

Under the cost of completion remedy, the injured promisee is entitled to money damages for the cost of completing the promise, less the unpaid portion of the contract price, if any.

For example, B hires A to build a house for $100,000 but A fails to perform as required by their contract. B then has to hire C to build the house for $150,000. Under the cost of completion remedy, A would owe B $50,000 because this is the extra expense B had to pay to have the house built after A breached the contract.

2. The Diminution in Value Measure

If the cost of completion is grossly and unfairly out of proportion to the benefit to the promisee, the court may award the diminution in value remedy which awards the promisee the loss in not being in the position he or she would have been in if there had been no breach. The diminution in value remedy is not awarded as often as the cost of completion remedy except where there is substantial performance by the promisor plus economic waste. This is generally a lower recovery than the cost of completion remedy.

For example, A hires B to build a house. A specifies that B is to use only Type-1 pipe, however, B builds the house using Type-2 pipe. A sues B for breach of contract. The difference in the value between a house with Type-1 pipe and a house with Type-2 pipe is $500. In order for B to replace the pipes, B would have to tear down all of the interior walls of the house at a cost of approximately $20,000. This would be the cost of completion remedy. However, under the economic waste doctrine, the court would more likely award the diminution in value award because there was substantial performance and to require B to tear down all of the walls would be economically unfeasible.

Breach By Person Who Has Contracted To Have Services Performed

When there is a breach by the person who has contracted to have services performed, there are two basic measures of damages: (1) The Cost of Cover Measure; and (2) The Recovery of Damages Measure.

1. The Cost of Cover Measure

The cost of cover measure provides that the non-breaching party be awarded the amount necessary to pay for substitute performance.

2. The Recovery of Damages Measure

For example, if A contracts to have B build a house, and then B commits a total breach, A can recover the cost of the entire contract price.

Miscellaneous Damages

Incidental Damages

Incidental damages refers to the cost of arranging for the substitute performance. For example, using the foregoing fact pattern, incidental damages may include the cost of additional attorney fees to negotiate the new contract between B the new builder.

Mitigation of Damages

Mitigation refers to the deduction of damages which could have been mitigated by the non-breaching party.

For example, the general measure of recovery by a wrongfully discharged employee is the amount of his or her salary for the period of service during which the employee was wrongfully discharged, less the amount which the employer affirmatively proves the employee has earned, or with reasonable effort might have earned, from other employment.

The general rule concerning mitigation in connection with the breach of an employment contract is that you don't have to mitigate damages by accepting inferior and different employment. However, if you do accept employment for the period of wrongful discharge, the amount you earn during that period of time reduces the damages as long as the employment accepted is in the same field as where the breach occurred.

Liquidated Damages

Liquidated damages are those damages which were negotiated and agreed to in the contract. Liquidated damages will serve as the measure of damages for a breach of the contract if the following applies:

1. At the time of contract, damages were difficult to ascertain; and

2. Damages are reasonable in light of the harm which occurred from the breach.

Damages Under Quasi-Contracts

Damages may be assessed under certain circumstances even if there was no contract. This would occur where a party either incurred a benefit or suffered a detriment, e.g. incurred a cost.

For example, A agrees to pay $500 to B to drive her son, C, to his grandmother's house across country. This is not a contract, but an offer to make a unilateral contract. Acceptance requires complete performance, i.e., B must accomplish driving C across country. If B starts the trip with C, but is called back by A, there is no contract because complete performance has not yet occurred. However, B may have still incurred a detriment in preparing for the trip. A may be required to pay B his costs on a theory of quasi-contract.

Specific Performance

Specific performance is a remedy available to an aggrieved party who would not be adequately made whole with money damages. Instead, the party seeks wants the contract enforced. Whenever the subject matter of the contract is unique, such as real property, specific performance is an authorized equitable remedy which the court can award at its own discretion.

For example, if A contracts with B to sell B a certain piece of land, but A later changes his mind, B can petition the court to force A to sell the land.

Although they can be considered unique, personal services contracts -- such as an entertainment contract -- cannot be specifically performed. However, the non-breaching party may be able to get an injunction, i.e. a court order that would prevent the breaching party from entertaining elsewhere, during the term of the contract that was breached.

For example, Singer signed a contract with Nightclub Owner to perform nightly in the club during the month of July at a salary of $500 per week. Shortly after signing the contract, Singer is offered another contract by Hotel Owner which would pay singer $1,000 per week to sing in the hotel lounge during the same month. Singer breaches his agreement with Nightclub Owner and signs the contract with Hotel Owner. Nightclub Owner would not be able to force Singer to sing in his establishment, however, Nightclub Owner could seek an injunction against Singer which would prevent Singer from performing for Hotel Owner during the month of July.

Arbitration

Parties may include a provision in the contract to have any disputes arising under the contract resolved through the arbitration process rather than by the court. Arbitration is less costly and less time consuming than litigation. The parties to the contract choose the arbitrator. They may choose one arbitrator or may elect to choose a panel of three arbitrators. In that case, each of the parties selects their one arbitrator and the third arbitrator is selected by the first two arbitrators.

The parties may provide that all disputes under the contract may be submitted to arbitration, or they can specify with particularity the terms of the contract which may be resolved through arbitration.

The American Arbitration Association recommends that a contract arbitration clause be included in commercial contracts. A sample agreement to submit a dispute to arbitration and a sample contract arbitration clause are set forth in the Appendix.

CHAPTER 8: CLASSIFICATION OF CONTRACTS

Contracts are classified according to certain prominent elements contained within the contract. Some of the most common contract classifications are set forth below.

Divisible and Indivisible Contracts

(a) Divisible Contract

A divisible contract is one which is composed of several independent clauses, the performance of any of which will bind the other party to some degree.

(b) Indivisible Contract

An indivisible contract is one which requires performance of every part of the contract as a condition precedent to binding the other party.

Executed and Executory Contracts

(a) Executed Contract

An executed contract refers to a contract which has already been completed. For example, if a Seller sells and delivers an item to Buyer and Buyer pays Seller at the same time, the transaction has taken place and both parties have performed.

(b) Executory Contract

An executory contract refers to a contract which has not yet been completed. For example, if Builder agrees to build an extension on Homeowner's house the following summer, this is an executory contract because performance is to be undertaken at some point in the future.

Express and Implied-in-Fact Contracts

(a) Express Contract

An express contract is one where the parties to the contract either put their mutual promises in writing, or expressly state their promises to one another.

For example, A agrees to sell his car to B for $500. B agrees to pay $500 to A in exchange for A's car.

(b) Implied-In-Fact Contract

An implied contract is one where the conduct of one of the parties implies his or her consent to enter into the contract.

For example, if a homeowner sits back and watches his driveway being repaved by a workman who is mistakenly working on the wrong driveway, it may be implied by the court that the homeowner exhibited the requisite intent to enter into a contract. In that case, an implied-in-fact contract may be found to exist, and the homeowner would be liable for the cost of the repaving.

Gratuitous and Onerous Contracts

(a) Gratuitous Contract

A gratuitous contract is generally not a legally enforceable contract because the promisor does not require any consideration in return for his promise to do or refrain from doing something.

For example, A tells his grandson B that he is A's favorite grandson and, therefore, A promises to give B $20,000 when B reaches the age of 21. When B reaches the age of 21, A reneges on the promise. B attempts to enforce the promise. The court will likely find that the promise was gratuitous and unenforceable.

(b) Onerous Contract

A contract is onerous when it is unreasonably burdensome or one-sided in that something is promised or given as consideration which in turn imposes a condition or obligation which is clearly unequal in value to what was promised or given.

Unilateral and Bilateral Contracts

(a) Unilateral Contract

A unilateral contract is basically a one-sided agreement whereby one party makes a promise to do -- or to refrain from doing -- something, in return for performance by the other party instead of a promise. Thus, the only time you can have a unilateral contract is where the offeror clearly states that the only way the offeree can accept the offer is to perform.

For example, A promises to pay B $500 if B drives A's car from New York to Florida. A clearly states that the only way B can accept A's offer is to accomplish driving the car to Florida. Thus, B must perform, i.e., drive A's car to Florida, in order to accept the contract and obligate A to pay B the $500.

A public offer is always unilateral. For example, A loses her diamond earrings and places an advertisement in the local newspaper offering a $50 reward to anyone who returns the earrings. In that case, the only way a person can claim the reward is if they actually perform, i.e. find and return the diamond earrings.

(b) Bilateral Contract

A bilateral contract exists when there are mutual promises be both parties to the contract, thus making each party both a promisor and a promisee. At the time of formation of a bilateral contract, the parties have not yet performed under the contract, but have merely promised to perform.

For example, a contract for the sale of real estate is a type of bilateral contract. The real estate contract represents the seller's promise to transfer the property to the buyer, and the buyer's promise to pay the seller a certain sum of money for the property which is the subject of the contract.

Void and Voidable Contracts

(a) Void Contract

A void contract is a contract which does not create a legal obligation because it did not have any legal existence or effect from its inception, such as where the contract lacked some essential element required in the making of a contract.

(b) Voidable Contract

A voidable contract is one which is void and not enforceable by the wrongdoer but is only made void and unenforceable by the innocent party if he or she so elects.

For example, if a minor enters into a contract with an adult, the contract is voidable only at the election of the minor.

Option Contract

An option contract exists when the offeror accepts consideration in exchange for his promise to keep the offer open for a designated period of time. The offer is thus irrevocable for that period of time. In most cases, the option contract must be supported by consideration. A sample option contract is set forth in the Appendix.

Certain option contracts may be formed without consideration. For example, a written offer, signed by the offeror, which recites a purported consideration for the making of the offer, and which proposes an exchange on fair terms within a reasonable period of time, may be formed without consideration. In addition, an offer which the offeror expects will induce substantial action or forbearance by the offeree prior to acceptance -- and which does induce such action or forbearance -- may be enforceable as an option contract so as to promote justice.

As more fully discussed in Chapter 10, option contracts under the UCC are enforceable without consideration if the statutory requirements are met.

Guaranty

A guaranty is a promise made by one person to pay a contractual obligation on behalf of another person if the other fails to perform

CLASSIFICATION OF CONTRACTS

the contractual obligation. The guarantor is more commonly referred to as a cosigner. In order for a guaranty to be enforceable, it must be in writing and signed by the guarantor.

For example, A wants to buy a car but does not earn enough income to qualify for financing. B agrees to be the guarantor for the loan by cosigning. Thus, if A ever defaults on the payments, the loan company can enforce the guaranty and seek payment directly from B.

A sample Guaranty is set forth in the Appendix.

CHAPTER 9: NON-PARTY RIGHTS

In General

Non-party rights are those rights given to persons who are not parties to the contract, but who are indirectly entitled to the benefits under the contract. The three basic types of non-party rights involve (1) third party beneficiaries; (2) assignments; and (3) delegations.

Third Party Beneficiaries

A third party beneficiary is one for whose benefit a promise is made in a contract, but who is not a party to the contract.

In order to determine whether a person is a third party beneficiary, you must examine the contract and determine if any of the promises contained in the contract inures to the benefit of a third party. If so, that person is considered a third party beneficiary to the contract and may be entitled to enforce his or her rights under the contract.

Intended vs. Incidental Beneficiaries

You must also determine whether the third party beneficiary is an intended beneficiary or an incidental beneficiary of the contract. In order for the third party beneficiary to have rights under the contract, he or she must be an intended beneficiary.

There are three criteria which must exist for the beneficiary to be deemed an intended beneficiary: (a) the third party must be identified in the promise; (b) the promise must run directly to the beneficiary; and (c) there must be a relationship between the promisee and the beneficiary that would support the intention to benefit.

> For example, A promises to pay B the sum of $1,000 if B will repair C's roof. B promises to repair the roof. In this scenario, A is the promisor and B is the promisee, and both are parties to the contract. However, C is receiving the benefit of the promise because it is C's roof which is being

repaired. Thus, C is the intended third party beneficiary of the contract and can enforce the contract against B.

If it is determined that the beneficiary is merely incidental, he or she has no rights under the terms of the contract. Using the foregoing example, an incidental beneficiary of the contract would be the supplier of the roofing materials used to repair C's roof. If B breaches the contract with A, the supplier has no right to sue B under the contract between A and B.

Creditor vs. Donee Beneficiaries

A third party beneficiary may be either a creditor or donee beneficiary. Most beneficiaries are donees, i.e., the benefit the beneficiary receives under the contract is a gift. If, however, the promisor is using the third party promise to satisfy an existing obligation already owed to the beneficiary, then the beneficiary is known as a creditor beneficiary.

> For example, using the foregoing fact pattern, C would be considered a donee beneficiary. However, if A owed C $500, but instead of repaying the money to C, A hired B to repair C's roof to satisfy the debt, C would be considered a creditor beneficiary.

Enforceability

The beneficiary may enforce the promise contained in the contract when his or her rights vest, that is, when the beneficiary learns about the promise and assents to it. Until vesting occurs, the promisor and promisee can change the contract in any way.

For example, again using the foregoing fact pattern, if A notified B that A had to cancel the contract to repair C's roof, before C knew about the contract, although C subsequently discovers that there had been such a contract, C cannot enforce the contract against B because C's rights never vested.

A creditor beneficiary can enforce the promise against either (a) the promisor based on the third party promise, or (b) the promisee based on the underlying obligation that was supposed to be satisfied. Using the previous example, A, the promisee, owes C, the third party beneficiary, the sum of $500. A pays B to fix C's roof and B promises to do so. If B doesn't fix C's roof, C has the option of (i) suing B on the basis of his promise to fix the roof or (ii) suing A for the underlying obligation -- the debt of $500.

Assignments

An assignment is basically a method of transferring virtually any kind of interest one may have to a third party, such as the assignment of the right to collect on a debt or an assignment of the right to receive some other source of money, such as income or inheritance funds. An assignment also exists when one party to a contract--known as the assignor--assigns his or her rights under the contract to a third party--the assignee.

> For example, A entered into an option contract to buy a car from B for the sum of $5,000. A can assign the right to buy the car to C; thus, C, a stranger to the contract between A and B, becomes an assignee. A sample contract assignment based on the this fact pattern is set forth in the Appendix.

Assignees are strangers to the underlying contract but are parties to the contract of assignment. An assignment is generally given in exchange for some type of consideration, such as money.

Upon assignment of a right, new labels are given to the parties, as follows:

> 1. Assignor - The person originally entitled to receive the right under the contract. The assignor no longer owns the right after he or she transfers it to the assignee.

> 2. Assignee - The person who is now entitled to receive the right as a result of a proper assignment. The assignee becomes the real party in interest and is entitled to enforce the right.

3. Obligor - The person who owes performance of the right being assigned. The obligor now must perform for the assignee instead of the assignor.

For example, A assigns his option to buy B's car to C. A is the assignor because A was originally entitled to buy B's car. C is the assignee because C received the right to buy B's car from A. B is the obligor because B owes performance in that he must sell his car to C.

Restrictions on Assignability

Most rights are assignable as there is a strong public policy in favor of assignability. However, there exist certain situations in which assignment of rights may be restricted, as follows:

(a) The Contract Prohibits Assignment - If the contract states that the rights under the contract may not be assigned, assignability is restricted but the power to assign may not necessarily be destroyed. However, breach of the non-assignment clause may cause the assignor to be liable for damages. Nevertheless, because the UCC favors assignability, such a clause may be unenforceable and thus a breach could not exist.

(b) The Law Prohibits Assignment - If assignment is prohibited by law, the assignment will not be enforceable.

(c) Personal Services - If the right involves performance of personal services, one must determine whether assignment of the right will substantially change the character or nature of performance. If so, the right may not be assignable. For example, if A contracts with B to act as a housekeeper for A's 2 bedroom apartment, A may not assign his right to B's housekeeping services to C, who owns a 20 room mansion.

Method of Assignment

In order to properly assign a right, there must be a description of the right to be assigned and words of present transfer. However, this does not mean that performance must be presently undertaken.

An example of a clause which designates a present assignment of a future right is , "I hereby assign my right to receive $100 from Mr. Jones three months from this date to my friend, John."

Enforceability

If the assignee is unable to enforce his or her right, the assignee has the option to sue the assignor for breach of warranty of assignability. For example, if A's option to buy B's car was contractually unassignable and C is unable to enforce his right to purchase the car from B, C can sue A.

Other problems relating to assignments may arise due to the fact that the assignor is still the apparent owner of the contractual right because his or her name is still on the contract. For example, the assignor may continue to deal with the obligor concerning the right. In that case, the obligor is free, without liability, to deal with the assignor until the obligor gets notice of the assignment. Once the obligor receives such notice, he can no longer deal with the assignor or he may be held liable to the assignee.

In addition, an unscrupulous assignor may attempt to assign the same right to other assignees thus creating multiple assignments. Generally, there are two rules which apply in this situation:

1. Gratuitous Assignments Rule - Gratuitous assignments are automatically revoked by a reassignment unless (a) there has been a writing delivered to the gratuitous assignee; or (b) indicia of ownership was delivered to the gratuitous assignee; or (c) promissory estoppel--also known as detrimental reliance--applies such that the gratuitous assignee detrimentally relied on the right.

2. First in Time First in Right Rule - If there are multiple unrevoked assignees, the first valid unrevoked assignment will generally prevail unless a subsequent assignee, without knowledge of the others, gets to the obligor first and gets either a (a) judgment; (b) payment; (c) indicia of ownership; or (d) a novation. Simple notice to the obligor is not sufficient in this case.

Delegations

As with assignments, there is a strong public policy in favor of delegation. A delegation exists when a party to the contract--the delegator--delegates a duty under the contract to a third party--the delegatee. Delegatees, like assignees, are strangers to the contract.

As in the foregoing example when A assigns his right to purchase B's car for the sum of $5,000 to C, A is also delegating the duty to pay the purchase price to C, thus C, a stranger to the contract between A and B, becomes a delegatee.

Upon delegation of a duty, new labels are given to the parties, as follows:

1. Delegator - The person who originally owed the duty. Nevertheless, the delegator remains liable to the obligee for the performance of the duty under the contract.

2. Delegatee - The person who assumes the duty from the delegator.

3. Obligee - The person who is entitled to receive performance of the delegated duty.

Enforceability

The delegator remains liable to the obligee for the performance of the duty under the contract, thus, if the delegatee fails to perform, the delegator must perform. As long as the duty is delegable, the obligee must accept the performance of the delegatee. The obligee's right to enforce the duty against the delegatee depends on whether the delegation was gratuitous or made for consideration, as follows:

1. Gratuitous Delegation - If the delegation is gratuitous, the obligee may not force the delegatee to perform and must sue the delegator for performance.

2. Delegation Made for Consideration - If the delegation was made for consideration, the obligee may force the delegatee to perform as well. The delegatee makes the promise

to the delegator to assume the duty to the obligee, thus, there is a third party promise. The obligee is a third party beneficiary of that promise. In that case, the obligee can sue either the delegator for breach of the original contract, or the delegatee for breach of the third party promise.

Novation

A novation is a contract whereby the obligee agrees to discharge the delegator from further obligation under the contract, in exchange for the delegatee promise to perform.

For example, A has a credit obligation of $50 to a local merchant. B agrees to assume A's debt to Merchant, thus creating a third party promise. Thus, Merchant may enforce the agreement against A, the delegatee, or against B, the original obligor. If A wants to be free of this obligation to Merchant, Merchant must enter into a novation contract with A, which would discharge A from any further obligation. If Merchant and A entered into a novation contract, Merchant would thereafter only be able to enforce the agreement against B.

CHAPTER 10: THE UNIFORM COMMERCIAL CODE (UCC)

In General

The Uniform Commercial Code (UCC) refers to the set of laws drafted by the National Conference of Commissioners on Uniform State Laws. Congress has not enacted the UCC as a federal law except for the District of Columbia. The purpose underlying the drafting of a uniform set of laws dealing with commercial transactions was to promote certainty and predictability of commercial law and, thus, reduce the number of legal disputes arising out of commercial matters.

It was recognized that it would be particularly advantageous if the UCC were uniformly adopted by all of the states with little or no revision or amendment. Nevertheless, all of the states have adopted some form of the UCC, along with numerous jurisdictional amendments. Thus, uniformity as it relates to the laws of the various states is somewhat of a misnomer.

The UCC contains eleven general articles governing commercial transactions:

Article 1: General Provisions

Article 2: Sales

Article 3: Commercial paper

Article 4: Bank Deposits and Collections

Article 5: Letters of Credit

Article 6: Bulk Transfers

Article 7: Warehouse Receipts, Bills of Lading and Other Documents of Title

Article 8: Investment Securities

Article 9: Secured Transactions; Sales of Accounts and Chattel Paper

Article 10: Effective Date and Repealer

Article 11: Effective Date and Transition Provisions

The UCC does not claim to be a comprehensive set of commercial laws. For example, there are certain purportedly commercial matters which are not addressed by the UCC, such as the sale of real property, insurance contracts, bankruptcy matters, and suretyship transactions. Such matters are left to the jurisdiction of general contract law. In addition, certain matters which are covered by the UCC must still rely on non-UCC law for support, guidance and clarification. In addition, where there is a federal law which conflicts with a UCC provision, the federal law will prevail over the UCC.

Offer

In General

In order to be a valid offer, a contract governed by the UCC, except in certain cases, need only provide the quantity of items to be sold. For example, Merchant offers to buy 10,000 pencils from Supplier. Supplier agrees to sell Merchant 10,000 pencils. No other terms are mentioned. After receiving the merchandise, Merchant fails to pay Supplier for the pencils. Supplier sues. The court may award Supplier the reasonable cost of the pencils, even though no price was specified. If Merchant and Supplier had previous transactions for the sale of pencils, the Court will likely use this figure as the cost of the pencils.

Total Output and Requirements Contracts

Section 2-306(1) of the UCC sets forth an exception to the rule requiring the contract to recite the quantity of items to be sold. Such an exception exists when a contract for the sale of goods calls for Buyer's purchase of the "total output" of the Seller (an "output" contract), or when the contract calls for Buyer's promise to purchase "all the product that Buyer requires" from the Seller (a "requirements" contract).

In that case, a "reasonable" quantity will be implied by the court should there be a dispute. If there has been a stated estimate, the Court may use this as a guideline to determine a good faith quantity. If there is no stated estimate, the Court may consider the terms of prior output contracts between the parties.

Firm Offer

A merchant's firm offer is defined in Section 2-205 of the UCC as an offer by a merchant to buy or sell goods in a signed writing which, by its terms, gives assurance that it will be held open.

> For example, Merchant makes the following offer to Buyer: "I am offering apples at $10 per bushel. I will hold this offer open for 60 days from the date of this notice. Signed, Merchant." This is a merchant's firm offer because it is a signed writing which states that the offer will be held open. If the offer had simply stated "I am offering apples at $10 per bushel. Signed, Merchant." This would not constitute a "firm offer" because it does not contain any assurance that the offer would be held open.

If the assurance is supplied by the offeree, the writing must also be signed by the offeror in order to make it a binding firm offer.

> For example, Merchant states: "I am offering apples at $10 per bushel. Signed, Merchant." Buyer responds: "I received your firm offer for the sale of apples at $10 per bushel, and confirm that we may accept at any time within the next 30 days. Signed, Buyer." Merchant's offer was not a firm offer because it contained no assurance that the offer would be held open. Since Buyer's writing contained the assurance, in order to be enforceable against Merchant as a firm offer, Merchant must sign Buyer's writing acknowledging the assurance.

The merchant's firm offer is not revocable during the time stated in the writing. However, if there is no time stated in the writing, the offer will be deemed irrevocable for a reasonable period of time. In either case, despite what the writing may state, the period of irrevocability may not exceed three months.

> For example, Merchant states: "I am offering apples at $10 per bushel. I will hold this offer open for 3 months from the date of this notice. Signed, Merchant." This offer is thus irrevocable for 3 months. Nevertheless, if the Merchant had stated that the offer would be open for 120 days, the period of irrevocability would still be limited to 3 months according to the statute.

Unlike an option contract, which requires that the offeree give some consideration to hold an offer open for a stated period of time, the merchant's firm offer under the UCC does not require any consideration.

Acceptance

The offer contained in a contract involving the sale of goods, governed by the UCC, can be accepted by (1) a promise to buy goods, or (2) by performance.

> 1. Acceptance by a Promise to Buy Goods - A offers to buy corn from B, a farmer. To validly accept A's offer, B can simply call A and promise to send the shipment of corn.

> 2. Acceptance by Performance - Using the foregoing example, B can also validly accept A's offer by shipping the corn to A, an act which constitutes performance. In addition, there are certain rules which accompany acceptance by performance, as follows:

> (a) If performance will take some time, then notice that the performance will take place is required;

> (b) Acceptance occurs whether performance consisted of shipping the right goods or the wrong goods. The rationale for this is that we must make the shipment an acceptance of the offer so that there is a valid contract which can be declared to have been breached in order to provide the buyer

with a remedy at law against the seller of the non-conforming goods. Nevertheless, an exception to this rule exists when the seller states that the shipment of non-conforming goods is being sent as an accommodation to the buyer. In this case, the shipment of non-conforming goods is treated as a counter-offer which may or may not be accepted by the buyer. The counter-offer, in effect, rejects the original offer. If the buyer uses the non-conforming goods, he is deemed to have accepted the counter-offer and thus a contract is formed.

Counter-Offers

Under the UCC, counter-offers are limited to the following two methods:

1. By shipping non-conforming goods as an accommodation, as set forth above; or

2. By making words of acceptance expressly conditioned on a new or different term.

Modifications

Where the parties to a contract seek to modify the terms of the original contract, the modification would still be enforceable, even without consideration, as long as it was done in good faith, and new duties arise under the contract as a result.

Identified Goods

Casualty to identified goods e.g., when goods are destroyed, operates to discharge the duties under the contract. This is similar to the concept of impossibility in non-UCC contracts. The casualty must occur before the risk of loss has passed from seller to buyer.

Identified goods are those which are either:

1. Identified in the contract; or

2. Marked, shipped or otherwise designated as the goods under the contract.

Risk of Loss

Risk of loss passes from seller to buyer when the seller has completed performance under the contract, as follows:

1. Face-to-Face Delivery - If the seller is a merchant, the risk of loss passes upon physical receipt of the goods by the buyer. However, if the seller is not a merchant, then risk of loss occurs when tender of delivery occurs. For example, tender occurs when the seller notifies the buyer that the goods are available and makes the goods available to the buyer.

2. Delivery by Intermediary or Carrier - The risk of loss depends on how the goods are shipped:

a) FOB -- free on board -- to a stated destination, e.g. FOB New York. This means that the goods will be priced so freight to the destination is included. If the goods are sent FOB to a place other than where the seller is, it is known as a destination contract and the seller has an obligation to get the goods to the place and tender delivery by notice of availability and holding the goods for a reasonable time. If the goods are damaged or lost either before they reach the destination, or before the goods are at the destination for a reasonable time, the duties are discharged. However, if the goods are at the destination for a reasonable time after buyer is notified, and they are lost or damaged, it is the buyer's problem and he must pay for the goods anyway.

b) FAS -- free along side -- Port - This means that the price of the goods includes delivery to the port or ship.

c) CIF (cost-insurance-freight) Port

d) C&F (cost and freight) Port

For all of the above examples except FOB to a destination other than where the seller is, the general risk of loss rule is that the risk of loss will pass when the Seller delivers the goods to the carrier and makes a reasonable contract for their delivery. This ends the seller's responsibility. If there is casualty before delivery of the goods to the carrier, then the duties are discharged. However, if there is casualty after delivery of the goods to the carrier, it is the Buyer's problem and he still must pay for the goods.

Where partial casualty of the shipment occurs, the buyer has the option of either (1) treating the contract as terminated; or (2) electing to take the goods with a price adjustment.

Performance

Under the UCC, if there is a single delivery of goods, the duty to deliver must be undertaken perfectly. Nevertheless, the UCC provides that if tender is not perfect, the seller has the right to cure tender anytime up to the agreed upon time of performance.

For example, if Farmer is required to deliver 1000 chickens by February 1st, but instead delivers 999 by January 31st, he has 1 more day to comply and deliver the last chicken.

Nevertheless, if a prior course of dealing can be shown which indicates that partial delivery has always been acceptable, then Farmer must be given some reasonable time to cure.

Breach Of Contract

The remedies available for breach of contract under the UCC are similar to non-UCC remedies, however, they are given different labels.

Seller's "Status Quo" Remedies

1. If during manufacture, seller manufactures and buyer breaches, seller is entitled to do anything reasonable, e.g. continue to manufacture goods and sell as a finished products;

2. If the seller has shipped goods in transit to buyer and buyer breaches, seller can stop the goods in transit. This applies to all goods if the buyer is insolvent so the goods won't be delivered and get into the hands of the buyer's creditors. However, if buyer is merely breaching, then the seller can only stop large shipments.

3. If the goods are already delivered, and the buyer breaches, if the buyer is insolvent, the seller may reclaim the goods within 10 days after delivery. If the buyer is not insolvent, the seller must sue for breach of contract.

Seller's "Right of Resale" Remedies

1. The seller has the right to find a substitute buyer to buy the goods. To exercise that right, the seller is required to give the buyer notice of intention to resell the goods. That notice is excused if the goods will perish or decline speedily. The seller must also make a commercially reasonable resale. If there is a resale, the seller is entitled to recover the difference between the contract price and the resale price from the buyer.

2. If there is no resale, the seller can get a market price recovery standard of damages, which would be the difference between the contract price and the market price for the goods at the time and place of tender.

3. Sellers who sell goods for the same price all of the time and who, therefore, experience no change in market price rendering the above two remedies ineffective, can sue the buyer for the profit they would have made on the sale (lost volume sales).

4. Seller can sue the buyer for the price of the goods whenever the goods are so unique that there is no resale value or market price. The seller will then give the buyer the goods. This is similar to specific performance in non-UCC contracts.

Buyer's "Status Quo" Remedies

1. The buyer can reject nonconforming goods anytime before the buyer accepts the goods.

2. The buyer can revoke acceptance of the goods if the buyer thereafter realizes that there is a defect with the goods. However, the defect must be substantial because acceptance has already been taken. In addition, the defect must have been difficult to discover.

Buyer's Procedures to Exercise Remedies

1. The buyer must give the seller notice of the defect. Once the notice is given, the buyer must wait for seller's instructions. If seller gives reasonable instructions, buyer must follow them. However, if the seller does not give any instructions, or gives unreasonable instructions, then the buyer can do anything reasonable with the goods at the seller's expense (e.g. sell the goods, return the goods, etc.).

2. The buyer must attempt to cover his losses, i.e., the buyer must go out into the market place without unreasonable delay to buy a reasonable substitute for the goods. If the buyer does that, he is entitled to receive the difference between the cost of covering the goods, and the contract price, so that the buyer is "made whole."

3. To determine a market price recovery, the buyer gets the difference between the market price when the buyer learns of the breach and the contract price.

4. Whenever the subject matter of the contract is unique, the Buyer can sue the seller to require that the goods be delivered.

The Statute of Frauds

In General

Section 2-201 of the UCC sets forth the Code's statute of frauds, which requires that there be some writing sufficient to indicate that a contract for the sale of goods was entered into by the parties, and signed by the party against whom enforcement is sought. The statute applies to the sale of goods with a value of $500 or over. The writing must recite a quantity term. If such a writing is produced, the contract may be enforced, but only for the quantity of goods shown in the writing.

Notwithstanding the foregoing requirements pertaining to the sufficiency of the writing, Section 2-201 also states that a written confirmation between merchants, which is signed by the sender, and which recites a quantity term, need not be signed by the party to be charged in order to be enforceable. If the receiving party does not want the goods, it is incumbent upon him to send a written notice of objection to the seller within 10 days after the written confirmation is received.

Exceptions

Section 2-201 also sets forth the exceptions to the writing requirement. If the contract does not satisfy the writing requirement, it may still be valid and enforceable under the following conditions:

1. If the goods are specially manufactured for the buyer and the seller has substantially begun production or procurement of the goods prior to receiving a notice of repudiation from the buyer; or

2. If the party who is being charged makes an admission in court, by pleadings, testimony or otherwise, that a contract for sale was made; or

3. If the goods have been received and accepted, or if payment for the goods has been made and accepted.

The Parol Evidence Rule

In General

Section 2-202 of the UCC sets forth the Code's version of the Parol Evidence Rule, which states that the terms of a final written agreement, or confirmatory memoranda between the parties, may not be contradicted by evidence of any prior agreement or contemporaneous oral agreement.

Exceptions

The Code does allow the parties to explain or supplement the writing by introducing evidence involving:

Course of Dealing - Course of dealing refers to the sequence of previous conduct between the parties to a particular transaction which is fairly to be regarded as establishing a common basis of understanding for interpreting their expressions and other conduct (UCC Section 1-205(1));

Usage of Trade - Usage of trade refers to any practice or method of dealing having such regularity of observance in a place, vocation or trade as to justify an expectation that it will be observed with respect to the transaction in question (UCC Section 1-205(2)).

Course of Performance - Course of performance shall be relevant where the contract for sale involves repeated occasions for performance by either party with knowledge of the nature of the performance and opportunity for objection to it by the other, where such course of performance was accepted or acquiesced in without objection (UCC Section 2-208(1)).

Unconscionability

Section 2-302 of the UCC sets forth the Code's definition of unconscionability which states that a contract may not be enforced if the court finds the contract, or any clause of the contract, to have been unconscionable at the time it was made. The court also has the option of enforcing the remainder of the contract without the unconscionable clause, or placing a limitation on the unconscionable clause to avoid an unconscionable result from its application. The parties to the contract are permitted to introduce evidence to show that the contract, or clause of the contract, are not unconscionable.

APPENDIX 1: ANALYSIS OF A SIMPLE CONTRACT

Using the information contained in this almanac, following is an analysis of the terms and conditions of the simple contract set forth below.

CONSTRUCTION AGREEMENT

THIS AGREEMENT is hereby entered into this 1st day of January, 1994, between Mary Jones, of 123 Main Street, City, State 10000 ("Homeowner"), and Build-A-Deck Contractors, of 456 Center Street, City, State 10000 ("Contractor").

The above parties, for the consideration set forth below, hereby agree as follows:

1. Contractor agrees to build a deck for Homeowner in the exact dimensions and specifications set forth on the attached Exhibit A, which is made a part of this agreement.

2. Contractor agrees to provide and pay for all labor and materials necessary to complete the deck.

3. Homeowner agrees to pay Contractor the sum of Five Thousand ($5,000) Dollars as and for compensation for labor and materials, payable as follows:

(a) One Thousand ($1,000) upon signing this agreement; and

(b) Two Thousand ($2,000) when the deck is 50% completed; and

(c) Two Thousand ($2,000) upon completion of the deck.

4. Contractor agrees that they will begin work on the deck within seven (7) calendar days from the date the contract is signed; and that the deck shall be completed within forty-five (45) calendar days from the date of contract.

5. Homeowner and Contractor agree that time is of the essence in completion of this deck, therefore, if the deck is

not completed by the date set forth herein due to the neglect of the Contractor, Contractor agrees to pay Homeowner the sum of Twenty-Five ($25) per day as liquidated damages until such time as the work is completed.

6. Notwithstanding Paragraph 5 of this agreement, in the event Contractor is delayed from completing the deck due to an act of God, fire, flood or other unavoidable event, or by fault of Owner, the date of completion shall be extended accordingly.

7. This contract contains the entire understanding between Homeowner and Contractor and any changes to this contract must be in writing and signed by both parties.

8. This contract is not assignable without the written consent of both parties.

9. This contract is governed by the laws of the State of New York.

10. The invalidity, in whole or in part, of any term of this agreement does not affect the validity of the remainder of the agreement.

By: _____
Mary Jones, Homeowner

By: _____
Mr. John Smith, President
Build-A-Deck Contractors

APPENDIX 1

ANALYSIS OF THE AGREEMENT

CONSTRUCTION AGREEMENT

Analysis: This heading sets forth the description of the type of document you are creating and basically serves to identify the document. In this example, we are setting forth the terms of an agreement for the construction of a pool.

THIS AGREEMENT is hereby entered into this 1st day of January, 1994, between Mary Jones, of 123 Main Street, City, State 10000 ("Homeowner"), and Build-A-Deck Contractors, of 456 Center Street, City, State 10000 ("Contractor").

Analysis: This paragraph is known as the caption. It identifies the parties to the contract. Following the identification of the various parties, there is generally an indication of how the party is going to be identified throughout the agreement. For example, Mary Jones will thereafter be identified as ("Homeowner") throughout the agreement and Build-A-Deck Contractors will thereafter be identified as ("Contractor") throughout the agreement.

The above parties, for the consideration set forth below, hereby agree as follows:

The second paragraph contains the language indicating that the parties have entered into an agreement and recites the existence of consideration.

1. Contractor agrees to build a deck for Homeowner in the exact dimensions and specifications set forth on the attached Exhibit A, which is made a part of this agreement.

2. Contractor agrees to provide and pay for all labor and materials necessary to complete the deck.

3. Homeowner agrees to pay Contractor the sum of Five Thousand ($5,000) Dollars as and for compensation for labor and materials, payable as follows:

(a) One Thousand ($1,000) upon signing this agreement; and

(b) Two Thousand ($2,000) when the deck is 50% completed; and

(c) Two Thousand ($2,000) upon completion of the deck.

4. Contractor agrees that they will begin work on the deck within seven (7) calendar days from the date the contract is signed; and that the deck shall be completed within forty-five (45) calendar days from the date of contract.

> *Analysis*: Paragraphs #1 - #4 set forth the mutual promises by and between the parties. In addition, the promise to pay contained in Paragraph #3(a)-(c) made by Homeowner contains conditions precedent in that certain events must occur before the obligation to pay arises.

5. Homeowner and Contractor agree that time is of the essence in completion of this deck, therefore, if the deck is not completed by the date set forth herein due to the neglect of the Contractor, Contractor agrees to pay Homeowner the sum of Twenty-Five ($25) per day as liquidated damages until such time as the work is completed.

> *Analysis*: Paragraph #5 sets forth a liquidated damages clause which is invoked should the Contractor breach the timetable set forth in the Agreement. Provision of a liquidated damages clause allows the parties to the contract to agree at the time of contract what the damages will be should there be a breach.

6. Notwithstanding Paragraph #5 of this agreement, in the event Contractor is delayed from completing the deck due to an act of God, fire, flood or other unavoidable event, or by fault of Homeowner, the date of completion shall be extended accordingly.

> *Analysis*: Paragraph #6 sets forth the events which will excuse a breach, also known as a "force majeure" clause, and allows for an extension of the contract.

7. This contract contains the entire understanding between Owner and Contractor and any changes to this contract must be in writing and signed by both parties.

APPENDIX 1

Analysis: Paragraph #7 contains a merger clause which declares that the agreement is the final written understanding of the parties. This clause serves to excludes the introduction of parol evidence to prove that there were any enforceable provisions other than those contained in the written contract.

8. This contract is not assignable without the written consent of both parties.

Analysis: Paragraph # 8 provides that the contract is not unilaterally assignable and sets forth the requirement for assignment.

9. This contract is governed by the laws of the State of New York.

Analysis: Paragraph #9 sets forth the parties choice of law to be applied in case a dispute arises.

10. The invalidity, in whole or in part, of any term of this agreement does not affect the validity of the remainder of the agreement.

Analysis: Paragraph #10 sets forth the severability clause which declares that the agreement is enforceable whether or not one of the terms contained therein is deemed unenforceable or invalid.

The "closing" of the contract includes the signature lines for the parties to the contract. The signatures demonstrate that the parties have agreed to the terms of the contract. If not set forth elsewhere in the agreement, the closing may also set forth the addresses of the parties and the date that the agreement was signed.

APPENDIX 2: CAPACITY TO CONTRACT ACCORDING TO AGE

STATE	MINIMUM AGE TO CONTRACT	ALTERNATIVE
Alabama	19	Married or widowed and over 18
Alaska	19	Married
Arizona	18	None
Arkansas	18	With court authorization
California	18	Married; or active duty in the military; or living apart from parent or guardian with consent
Colorado	18	None
Connecticut	18	None
Delaware	18	None
District of Columbia	18	None
Florida	18	Married
Georgia	Married age 16 and over	
Hawaii	18	Married
Idaho	18	Married
Illinois	18	With court authorization
Indiana	18	None
Iowa	18	Married
Kansas	18	Married age 16 and over; or with court authorization
Kentucky	18	None
Louisiana	18	With court authorization; or 15 and over if emancipated
Maine	18	None
Maryland	18	None
Massachusetts	18	15 and over for life insurance; 16 and over for car insurance
Michigan	18	Married; or with court authorization; or active duty in military; or emancipation

STATE	MINIMUM AGE TO CONTRACT	ALTERNATIVE
Minnesota	18	None
Mississippi	21	Married age 18 or over; or with court authorization
Montana	18	None
Nebraska	19	Married
Nevada	18	None
New Hampshire	18	None
New Jersey	18	None
New Mexico	18	Married; or with court authorization; or active duty in the military; or living apart from parent or guardian with consent
New York	18	Married
North Carolina	18	None
North Dakota	18	Active duty in military; or emancipation
Ohio	18	None
Oklahoma	18	With court authorization
Oregon	18	With court authorization
Pennsylvania	18	None
Rhode Island	18	None
South Carolina	18	none
South Dakota	18	None
Tennessee	18	With court authorization
Texas	18	With court authorization
Utah	18	Married
Vermont	18	None
Virginia	18	None
Washington	18	Married and spouse of age
West Virginia	18	Married; or with court authorization
Wisconsin	18	None
Wyoming	19	With court authorization

APPENDIX 3: CONSUMER PROTECTION AGENCIES

STATE	ADDRESS	TELEPHONE NUMBER
Alabama	Consumer Protection Division, Office of the Attorney General, 11 S. Union Street, Montgomery, AL 36130	205-261-7334
Alaska	Consumer Protection Section, Office of the Attorney General, 1031 W. 4th Avenue, Suite 110-B, Anchorage, AK 99501	907-279-0428
Arizona	Financial Fraud Division, Office of the Attorney General, 1275 W. Washington St., Phoenix, AZ 85007	602-542-3702
Arkansas	Consumer Protection Division, Office of the Attorney General, 200 Tower Building, 4th & Center Streets, Little Rock, AR 72201	501-682-2007
California	Public Inquiry Unit, Office of the Attorney General, 1515 K Street., Suite 511, Sacramento, CA 94244-2550	916-322-3360
California	Consumer Protection Division, Los Angeles City Attorney's Office, 200 N. Main Street, 1600 City Hall East, Los Angeles, CA 90012	213-485-4515
Colorado	Consumer Protection Unit, Office of the Attorney General, 1525 Sherman Street, 3rd Floor, Denver, CO 80203	303-866-5167
Connecticut	Department of Consumer Protection, 165 Capitol Avenue, Hartford, CT 06106	203-566-4999
Delaware	Division of Consumer Affairs, Department of Community Affairs, 820 N. French Street, 4th Floor, Wilmington, DE 19801	302-571-3250
District of Columbia	Department of Consumer & Regulatory Affairs, 614 H Street NW, Washington, DC 20001	202-737-7000
Florida	Division of Consumer Services, 218 Mayo Building, Tallahassee, FL 32399	904-488-2226

STATE	ADDRESS	TELEPHONE NUMBER
Georgia	Governor's Office of Consumer Affairs, 2 Martin Luther King Jr. Drive SE, Plaza Level, E Tower, Atlanta, GA 30334	404-656-7000
Hawaii	Office of Consumer Protection, 828 Fort St. Mall, Honolulu, HI 96812-3767	808-548-2560
Idaho	None Listed	
Illinois	Consumer Protection Division, Office of the Attorney General, 100 W. Randolph Street, 12th Floor, Chicago, IL 60601	312-917-3580
Indiana	Consumer Protection Division, Office of the Attorney General, 219 State House, Indianapolis, IN 46204	37-232-6330
Iowa	Consumer Protection Division, Office of the Attorney General, 1300 E. Walnut Street, 2nd Floor, Des Moines, IA 50319	515-281-5926
Kansas	Consumer Protection Division, Office of the Attorney General, Kansas Judicial Center, 2nd Floor, Topeka, KS 66612	913-296-3761
Kentucky	Consumer Protection Division, Office of the Attorney General, 209 St. Clair Street, Frankfort, KY 40601	502-564-2200
Louisiana	Consumer Protection Section, Office of the Attorney General, State Capitol Building, P.O. Box 94005, Baton Rouge, LA 70804	504-342-7013
Maine	Consumer and Antitrust Division, Office of the Attorney General, State House Station #6, Augusta, ME 04333	207-289-3716
Maryland	Consumer Protection Division, Office of the Attorney General, 7 N. Calvert Street, 3rd Floor, Baltimore, MD 21202	301-528-8662
Massachusetts	Consumer Protection Division, Office of the Attorney General, One Ashburton Place, Room 1411, Boston, MA 02108	617-727-7780

APPENDIX 3

STATE	ADDRESS	TELEPHONE NUMBER
Michigan	Consumer Protection Division, Office of the Attorney General, 670 Law Building, Lansing, MI 48913	517-373-1140
Minnesota	Office of Consumer Services, Office of the Attorney General, 117 University Avenue, St. Paul, MN 55155	612-296-2331
Mississippi	Consumer Protection Division, Office of the Attorney General, P.O. Box 220, Jackson, MS 39205	601-359-3680
Missouri	Trade Offense Division, Office of the Attorney General, P.O. Box 899, Jefferson City, MO 65102	314-751-2616
Montana	Consumer Affairs Unit, Department of Commerce, 1424 9th Avenue, Helena, MT 59620	406-444-4312
Nebraska	Consumer Protection Division, Department of Justice, 2115 State Capitol, P.O. Box 98920, Lincoln, NE 68509	402-471-4723
Nevada	Department of Commerce, State Mail Room Complex, Las Vegas, NV 89158	702-486-4150
New Hampshire	Consumer Protection and Antitrust Division, Office of the Attorney General, State House Annex, Concord, NH 03301	603-271-3641
New Jersey	Division of Consumer Affairs, 1100 Raymond Boulevard, Room 504, Newark, NJ 07102	201-648-4010
New Mexico	Consumer and Economic Crime Division, Office of the Attorney General, P.O. Box Drawer 1508, Santa Fe, NM 87504	505-872-6910
New York	Consumer Protection Board, 99 Washington Avenue, Albany, NY 12210	518-474-8583
New York	Consumer Protection Board, 250 Broadway, 17th Floor, New York, NY 10007-2593	212-587-4908

STATE	ADDRESS	TELEPHONE NUMBER
North Carolina	Consumer Protection Section, Office of the Attorney General, P.O. Box 629, Raleigh, NC 27602	919-733-7741
North Dakota	Consumer Fraud Division, Office of the Attorney General, State Capitol Building, Bismarck, ND 58505	701-224-2210
Ohio	Consumer Frauds and Crimes Section, Office of the Attorney General, 30 E. Broad Street, 25th Floor, Columbus, OH 43266-0410	614-466-4986
Oklahoma	Consumer Affairs, Office of the Attorney General, 112 State Capitol Building, Oklahoma City, OK 73105	405-521-3921
Oregon	Financial Fraud Section, Office of the Attorney General, Justice Building, Salem, OR 97310	503-378-4320
Pennsylvania	Bureau of Consumer Protection, Office of the Attorney General, Strawberry Square, 14th Floor, Harrisburg, PA 17120	717-787-9707
Rhode Island	Consumer Protection Division, Office of the Attorney General, 72 Pine Street, Providence, RI 02903	401-277-2104
South Carolina	Department of Consumer Affairs, P.O. Box 5757, Columbia, SC 29250	803-734-9452
South Dakota	Division of Consumer Affairs, Office of the Attorney General, State Capitol Building, Pierre, SD 57501	605-773-4400
Tennessee	Division of Consumer Affairs, Department of Commerce & Insurance, 500 James Robertson Parkway, 5th Floor, Nashville, Tn 37219	615-741-4737
Texas	Consumer Protection Division, Office of the Attorney General, Box 12548, Capitol Station, Austin, TX 78711	512-463-2070

APPENDIX 3

STATE	ADDRESS	TELEPHONE NUMBER
Utah	Division of Consumer Protection, Department of Business Regulation, 160 E. Third South, P.O. Box 45802, Salt Lake City, UT 84145	801-530-6601
Vermont	Public Protection Division, Office of the Attorney General, 109 State Street, Montpelier, VT 05602	802-828-3171
Virginia	Division of Consumer Counsel, Office of the Attorney General, Supreme Court Building, 101 N. 8th Street, Richmond, VA 23219	804-786-2116
Washington	Consumer and Business Fair Practices Division, 710 2nd Avenue, Suite 1300, Seattle, WA 98104	206-464-7744
West Virginia	Consumer Protection Division, Office of the Attorney General, 812 Quarrier Street, 6th Floor, Charleston, WV 25301	304-348-8986
Wisconsin	Office of Consumer Protection, Department of Justice, P.O. Box 7856, Madison, WI 53707	608-266-1852
Wyoming	Office of the Attorney General, 123 State Capitol Building, Cheyenne, WY 82002	307-777-6286

APPENDIX 4: SAMPLE BREACH OF CONTRACT NOTIFICATION

March 1, 1994

Mary Jones
123 Main Street
City, State 10000

Mr. John Smith, President
Build-A-Deck Contractors
456 Center Street
City, State 10000

Re: Agreement Dated January 1, 1994

Dear Mr. Smith:

On January 1, 1994, we entered into a written agreement which provided that Build-A-Deck Contractors would build a deck for my home according to the specifications provided by me. A copy of the fully-executed agreement is attached hereto.

According to our agreement, you were to begin work on the deck no later than 7 calendar days following the execution of the agreement. Since the agreement was executed on January 1, 1994, work was to begin on the deck no later than January 8, 1994. Additionally, you were to complete work on the deck within 45 calendar days following the execution of the agreement, thus, the deck should have been completed on or before February 15, 1994.

Please take notice that you are now in breach of your obligations contained in that agreement in that as of this date, you have not begun work on the deck, and that this failure to comply with the terms of our agreement is due solely to the negligence of Build-A-Deck Contractors.

Please be further advised that I intend to hold you responsible for all actual and consequential damages arising from your breach, including but not limited to liquidated damages in the amount set forth in our agreement.

By:_____
Mary Jones, Homeowner

APPENDIX 5: SAMPLE STANDARD CONTRACT ARBITRATION CLAUSE

Any controversy or claim arising out of or relating to this contract, or the breach thereof, shall be settled by arbitration administered by the American Arbitration Association in accordance with its Commercial Arbitration Rules, and judgment on the award rendered by the arbitrator(s) may be entered in any court having jurisdiction thereof.[1]

---

[1] Source: A Guide to Arbitration for Business People, American Arbitration Association, 1992.

APPENDIX 6: SAMPLE AGREEMENT TO SUBMIT A DISPUTE TO ARBITRATION

We, the undersigned parties, hereby agree to submit to arbitration administered by the American Arbitration Association under its Commercial Arbitration Rules the following controversy: [describe nature of dispute].

We further agree that the above controversy be submitted to three arbitrators.

We further agree that we will faithfully observe this agreement and the rules, and that we will abide by and perform any award rendered by the arbitrators and that a judgment of the court having jurisdiction may be entered on the award.[1]

---

[1] Source: A Guide to Arbitration for Business People, American Arbitration Association, 1992.

APPENDIX 7: SAMPLE REAL ESTATE PURCHASE OPTION CONTRACT

THIS AGREEMENT is made this 1st day of January, 1995 by and between John Smith ("Seller") and Mary Jones ("Buyer"), as follows:

1. Buyer agrees to pay Seller the sum of $10,000, as consideration, for the option to purchase the real property owned by Seller located at 111 Main Street, Anytown, USA ("property").

2. This option is effective as of the date first written above and will remain in effect until January 1, 1996 ("option period"), at which time the option will expire if not previously exercised by Buyer.

3. Buyer hereby has the option and right to purchase said property during the option period stated herein for the sum of $100,000.

4. If Buyer exercises the option, the sum of $10,000 paid as consideration shall be applied to the purchase price stated in paragraph 2.

5. If Buyer elects to exercise his option to purchase said property within the option period, Buyer shall send written notification to Seller by certified or registered mail.

6. This option shall be binding upon and inure to the benefit of the parties, their successors and assigns.

By:_____
John Smith, Seller

By:_____
Mary Jones, Buyer

APPENDIX 8: SAMPLE GUARANTY

FOR GOOD AND VALUABLE CONSIDERATION, John Smith ("Guarantor"), agrees as follows:

1. Guarantor agrees that he is executing this guaranty as an inducement for ABC Appliances ("Lender") to extend credit to Mary Jones ("Borrower").

2. Guarantor unconditionally guarantees to Lender, the full and prompt payment of the following debt owed to Lender by Borrower:

> Borrower has entered into a financing agreement with Lender for the purchase of a refrigerator to be paid in six equal monthly installments of $100 per month, beginning on January 1, 1995, for a total purchase price of $600.

3. Guarantor agrees to remain bound on this guaranty notwithstanding any extension, renewal, forbearance, waiver, release, discharge or substitution of any collateral or security for the above referenced debt.

4. Guarantor agrees that in the event of a default by Borrower, Lender may seek payment directly from Guarantor.

5. Guarantor's obligation hereunder is limited to the debt herein described.

6. This guaranty shall be binding upon and inure to the benefit of the parties, their successors and assigns.

Dated:_____

By:_____
John Smith, Guarantor

APPENDIX 9: SAMPLE GENERAL ASSIGNMENT OF CONTRACT

LET IT BE KNOWN that, for value received, John Doe ("Assignor"), hereby assigns, transfers and sets over to Jane Smith ("Assignee"), all right, title and interest held by Assignor in and to a contract between Assignor and Mary Jones ("Seller") dated January 1, 1994 providing for the sale of a 1992 Ford Taurus automobile by Seller to Assignor for the sum of Ten Thousand ($10,000), as more fully set forth in said contract, a copy of which is attached hereto and made a part of this assignment.

Assignor hereby warrants and represents that said contract is fully assignable and in full force.

Assignee hereby assumes and agrees to perform all remaining obligations of Assignor under the contract, if any, and agrees to indemnify and hold Assignor harmless from any claim against Assignor arising from non-performance of the contract by Assignee.

Assignor further warrants that he has the full right and authority to transfer said contract, and that the rights herein transferred are free of lien and encumbrance of any kind whatsoever.

This assignment shall be binding upon and inure to the benefit of the parties, their successors and assigns.

Date:

By:_____
    John Doe, Assignor

By:_____
    Jane Smith, Assignee

APPENDIX 10: UNIFORM COMMERCIAL CODE - STATE ADOPTION OF ARTICLE 9 RELATING TO SALES AND SECURED TRANSACTIONS

STATE	EFFECTIVE DATE
Alabama	1/1/67
Alaska	1/1/63
Arizona	1/1/68
Arkansas	1/1/62
California	1/1/65
Colorado	7/1/65
Connecticut	10/1/61
Delaware	7/1/67
District of Columbia	1/1/65
Florida	1/1/67
Georgia	4/1/63
Hawaii	1/1/67
Idaho	1/1/68
Illinois	7/1/62
Indiana	7/1/64
Iowa	7/4/66
Kansas	1/1/66
Kentucky	7/2/60
Maine	12/31/64
Maryland	2/1/64
Massachusetts	10/1/58
Michigan	1/1/64
Minnesota	7/1/66
Mississippi	3/31/68
Montana	1/2/65
Nebraska	9/1/65
Nevada	3/1/67
New Hampshire	7/1/61
New Jersey	1/1/63
New Mexico	1/1/62
New York	9/27/64
North Carolina	7/1/67
North Dakota	7/1/66
Ohio	7/1/62
Oklahoma	1/1/63
Oregon	9/1/63
Pennsylvania	7/1/54
Rhode Island	1/2/62
South Carolina	1/1/68
South Dakota	7/1/67
Tennessee	7/1/64
Texas	7/1/66
Utah	1/1/66
Vermont	1/1/67

STATE	EFFECTIVE DATE
Virginia	1/1/66
Washington	7/1/67
West Virginia	7/1/64
Wisconsin	7/1/65
Wyoming	1/2/62

Note: Louisiana is the only state which has not yet adopted U.C.C. Article 9 due to the state's adherence to the Napoleonic Code.

GLOSSARY

Acceleration Clause - An acceleration clause is a provision or clause in a contract or document establishing that upon the occurrence of a certain event, such as a default in payments, a party's expected interest in the subject property will become prematurely vested.

Acceptance - Acceptance refers to one's consent to the terms of an offer, which consent creates a contract.

Accord and Satisfaction - Accord and satisfaction refers to the payment of money, or other thing of value, which is usually less than the amount owed or demanded, in exchange for extinguishment of the debt.

Actual Damages - Actual damages are those damages directly referable to the breach or tortious act and which can be readily proven to have been sustained and for which the injured party should be compensated as a matter of right. Also referred to as compensatory or general damages.

Adhesion Contract - An adhesion contract is a standardized contract form offered to consumers of goods and services on a take it or leave it" basis without affording the consumer a realistic opportunity to bargain, and under such conditions that the consumer cannot obtain the desired product or service except by acquiescing in form contract.

Agency - Agency is the relationship in which one person acts for or represents another by the latter's authority, such as principal and agent or proprietor and independent contractor relationships.

Agent - an agent is one who represents and acts for another under the contract or relation of agency.

Amortization Schedule - An amortization schedule is a plan for the payment of an indebtedness where there are partial payments of the principal and accrued interest, at stated periods for a definite time, upon the expiration of which the entire indebtedness will be extinguished.

Annual Percentage Rate (APR) - The annual percentage rate is the actual cost of borrowing money, expressed in the form of an annual rate to make it easy for one to compare the cost of borrowing money among several lenders.

Anticipatory Breach - An anticipatory breach is one a breach committed prior to the actual time of required performance which occurs when one party by declaration repudiates his contractual obligation before it is due.

Apparent Agency - Apparent agency refers to the situation when one person, whether or not authorized, reasonably appears to a third person, due to the manifestation of another, to be authorized to act as agent for such other.

Arbitration Clause - An arbitration clause is a clause inserted in a contract providing for compulsory arbitration in case of dispute as to the rights or liabilities under such contract.

Assignee - An assignee is a person to whom an assignment is made, also known as a grantee.

Assignment - An assignment is the transfer of an interest in a right or property from one party to another.

Attorney In Fact - An attorney-in-fact is an agent or representative of another given authority to act in that person's name and place pursuant to a document called a "power of attorney."

Bailee - A bailee is a person who holds the property of another for a specific purpose pursuant to an agreement between the parties known as a bailment contract.

Bailment - A bailment is the delivery of personal property to be held in trust for some special purpose, and upon a contract, express or implied, to conform with purpose of the trust.

GLOSSARY

Bailor - A bailor is a person who delivers personal property to another to be held in bailment.

Bankrupt - Bankrupt refers to the state or condition of one who is unable to pay his debts as they are, or become, due.

Bankruptcy - Bankruptcy is the legal process under federal law intended to insure fairness and equality among creditors of a bankrupt person, also known as a debtor, and to enable the debtor to start fresh by retaining certain property exempt from liabilities and unhampered by preexisting debts.

Bilateral Contract - A bilateral contract is one containing mutual promises between the parties to the contract, each being termed both a promisor and a promisee.

Boilerplate - Boilerplate refers to the standard or formal language found in legal documents of a given type, often in small print.

Bond - A bond is a certificate or other evidence of a debt on which the issuing company or governmental body promises to pay the bondholders a specified amount of interest for a specified length of time, and to repay the loan on the expiration date.

Breach of Contract - A breach of contract refers to the failure, without any legal excuse, to perform any promise which forms the whole or the part of a contract.

Capacity - Capacity is the legal qualification concerning the ability of one to understand the nature and effects of one's acts.

Collateral - Collateral is property which is pledged as security for the satisfaction of a debt.

Common Law - Common law is the system of jurisprudence which originated in England and was later applied in the United States. The common law is based on judicial precedent rather than statutory law.

Compensatory Damages - Compensatory damages are those damages directly referable to the breach or tortious act and which can be readily proven to have been sustained and for which the injured party should be compensated as a matter of right. Also referred to as actual or general damages.

Condition - A condition is a future and uncertain event upon the happening of which is made to depend the existence of an obligation.

Condition Concurrent - A condition concurrent is a condition precedent which exists only when parties to a contract are found to render performance at the same time.

Condition Precedent - A condition precedent is a condition which must occur before the agreement becomes effective and which calls for the happening of some event before the contract shall be binding on the parties.

Condition Subsequent - A condition subsequent is a provision giving one party the right to divest himself of liability and obligation to perform further if the other party fails to meet the condition.

Confession of Judgment - Confession of judgment refers to the entry of a judgment upon a written admission or confession of the debtor without the formality, time or expense of an ordinary legal proceeding.

Conflict of Laws - Conflict of laws is the body of law by which the court in which the action is maintained determines or chooses which law to apply where a diversity exists between the applicable law of that court's state, and the applicable law of another jurisdiction which has some interest in the controversy.

Consequential Damages - Consequential damages are those damages which are caused by an injury but which are not a necessary result of the injury and must be specially pleaded and proven in order to be awarded.

GLOSSARY

Conservator - A conservator is the court-appointed custodian of property belonging to a person determined to be unable to properly manage his property.

Consideration - Consideration is something of value given in return for a performance or promise of performance by another, for the purpose of forming a contract.

Contract - A contract is an agreement between two or more persons which creates an obligation to do or not to do a particular thing.

Conveyance - A conveyance is the transfer of property or title to property from one person to another by means of a written instrument and other formalities.

Counteroffer - A counteroffer is a statement by the offeree which has the legal effect of rejecting the offer and of proposing a new offer to the offeror.

Covenant - A covenant is an agreement or promise to do or not to do a particular thing as to bind oneself in contract.

Credit - Credit is that which is extended to the buyer or borrower on the seller or lender's belief that that which is given will be repaid.

Credit Report - A credit report refers to the document from a credit reporting agency setting forth a credit rating and pertinent financial data concerning a person or a company, which is used by banks, lenders, merchants, and suppliers in evaluating a credit risk.

Damages - In general, damages refers to monetary compensation which the law awards to one who has been injured by the actions of another, such as in the case of tortious conduct or breach of contractual obligations.

Default - Default is a failure to discharge a duty or do that which ought to be done.

Disclosure - Disclosure is the act of disclosing or revealing that which is secret or not fully understood. The Truth in Lending Act provides that there be disclosure to the consumer of certain information deemed basic to an intelligent assessment of a credit transaction.

Discount Rate - The discount rate is the percentage of the face amount of commercial paper which a holder pays when he transfers such paper to a financial institution for cash or credit.

Duress - Duress is action by one person which propels another person to do something he or she would not otherwise do.

Excuse - An excuse is a matter alleged as a reason for relief or exemption from some duty or obligation.

Executory Contract - An executory contract is a contract which has not yet been fully completed or performed.

Federal Trade Commission - The Federal Trade Commission is an agency of the federal government created in 1914 for the purpose of promoting free and fair competition in interstate commerce through the prevention of general trade restraints such as price-fixing agreements, false advertising, boycotts, illegal combinations of competitors and other unfair methods of competition.

Fiduciary - A fiduciary is a person having a legal duty, created by an undertaking, to act primarily for the benefit of another, in matters connected with the undertaking.

Finance Charge - A finance charge is any charge assessed for an extension of credit, including interest.

Force Majeure - Force majeure is a clause commonly found in construction contracts which protects the parties in the event that a part of the contract cannot be performed due to causes which are outside the control of the parties and could not be avoided by exercise of due care.

GLOSSARY

Foreclosure - Foreclosure refers to the procedure by which mortgaged property is sold on default of mortgagor in satisfaction of mortgage debt.

Fraud - Fraud is a false representation of a matter of fact, whether by words or by conduct, by false or misleading allegations, or by concealment of that which should have been disclosed, which deceives and is intended to deceive another so that he shall act upon it to his legal injury.

Free on Board (FOB) - Free on board is a commercial term that signifies a contractual agreement between a buyer and a seller to have the subject of a sale delivered to a designated place, usually either the place of shipment or the place of destination, without expense to the buyer.

Frustration of Purpose - Frustration of purpose in contract law occurs when an implied condition of an agreement does not occur or ceases to exist without fault of either party such that the absence of the implied condition frustrates one party intentions in making the agreement.

General Damages - General damages are those damages directly referable to the breach or tortious act and which can be readily proven to have been sustained and for which the injured party should be compensated as a matter of right. Also referred to as actual or compensatory damages.

Grace Period - The grace period is the period beyond the due date set forth in the contract during which time payment may be made without incurring a penalty.

Guarantor - A guarantor is one who makes a guaranty.

Guaranty - A guaranty is a promise to answer for the payment of another's debts, or the performance of another's duty, liability or obligation.

Impossibility - Impossibility is a defense to breach of contract and arises when performance is impossible due to the destruction of the subject matter of the contract or the death of a person necessary for performance.

Incapacity - Incapacity is a defense to breach of contract which refers to a lack of legal, physical or intellectual power to enter into a contract.

Indemnification Clause - An indemnification clause in a contract refers to the agreement by one party to secure the other party against loss or damage which may occur in the future in connection with performance of the contract.

Installment Contract - An installment contract is one in which the obligation, such as the payment of money, is divided into a series of successive performances over a period of time.

Interest - Interest is the compensation paid for the use of money loaned.

Joint and Several - Joint and several refers to the sharing of rights and liabilities among a group of people collectively and individually.

Judgment - A judgment is a final determination by a court of law concerning the rights of the parties to a lawsuit.

Letter of Intent - A letter of intent is a writing which sets forth the preliminary understanding of parties who wish to enter into a formal agreement. The letter of intent is not a contract and is not binding on the parties.

Liability - Liability refers to one's obligation to do or refrain from doing something, such as the payment of a debt.

Liquidated Damages - Liquidated damages refers to the amount stipulated by the parties to a contract representing a reasonable estimate of the damages which would result from a breach by the parties.

Loan Principal - The loan principal is the amount of the debt not including interest or any other additions.

Material Breach - A material breach refers to a substantial breach of contract which excuses further performance by the innocent party and gives rise to an action for breach of contract by that party.

Mediation - Mediation is a method of resolving disputes without court intervention by introducing a neutral third party to act as mediator between the parties.

Merger Clause - A merger clause is a provision in a contract which states that the written terms of the agreement may not be varied by prior or oral agreements because all such agreements are said to have merged into the writing.

Mitigation of Damages - Mitigation of damages refers to the duty imposed on an injured party to exercise reasonable diligence in attempting to minimize the damages resulting from the injury.

Mutual Agreement - Mutual agreement refers to the meeting of the minds of the parties to a contract concerning the subject matter of the contract.

Novation - A novation refers to the substitution of a new party and the discharge of an original party to a contract, with the assent of all parties.

Obligee - An obligee is one who is entitled to receive a sum of money or performance from the obligor.

Obligor - An obligor is one who promises to perform or pay a sum of money under a contract.

Offer - An offer is a manifestation of willingness to enter into a bargain which invites the acceptance of the person to whom the offer is made.

Offeree - An offeree is the person to whom an offer is made.

Offeror - An offeror is the person who makes an offer.

Option - An option is a right to purchase or lease property at an agreed upon price and terms within a specified time which is given for consideration.

Oral Agreement - An oral agreement is one which is not in writing or not signed by the parties.

Parol Evidence Rule - The parol evidence rule is the doctrine which holds that the written terms of an agreement may not be varied by prior or oral agreements.

Performance - Performance refers to the completion of one's contractual obligation.

Prepayment Penalty - A prepayment penalty is a penalty imposed on the borrower if a loan is paid before the due date.

Privity of Contract - Privity of contract refers to the relationship between the parties to a contract.

Purchase Order - A purchase order is a document which authorizes a seller to deliver goods and is considered an offer which is accepted upon delivery.

Quantum Meruit - Quantum meruit is an equitable doctrine based on unjust enrichment which refers to the extent of liability in a contract implied by law, also known as a quasi-contract, wherein the court infers a reasonable amount payable for goods and services even when there is no contract between the parties.

Quasi-Contract - Quasi contract refers to the legal obligation invoked in the absence of an agreement where there has been unjust enrichment.

Quid Pro Quo - Quid pro quo refers to the mutual consideration which passes between the parties to a contract rendering it valid and binding.

Reformation - Reformation is an equitable remedy which calls for the rewriting of a contract involving a mutual mistake or fraud.

Remedy - The remedy is the means by which a right is enforced or a violation of a right is compensated.

Repudiation - Repudiation refers to the refusal by one party to a contract to perform a duty or obligation owed to the other party.

Rescission - Rescission refers to the cancellation of a contract which returns the parties to the positions they were in before the contract was made.

Restatement of Contracts - The Restatement of Contracts is a series of volumes written and published by the American Law Institute (ALI) which attempts to state an orderly explanation of the current and evolving law of contracts, and sets forth a proposed direction which the ALI believes contract law should follow.

Restitution - Restitution refers to the act of restoring a party to a contract to their status quo, i.e., the position the party would have been in if no contract had been made.

Specific Performance - Specific performance is the equitable remedy available to an aggrieved party where there has been a breach of contract which requires the guilty party to perform his or her obligations under the contract.

Statute of Frauds - The Statute of Frauds refers to the requirement that certain contracts must be in writing to be legally enforceable.

Substantial Performance - Substantial performance refers to the performance of all of the essential terms of a contract so that the purpose of the contract has been accomplished giving rise to the right to compensation even though minor omissions may exist.

Successors - A successor is one who takes the place of another and continues in their position.

Surety - A surety is one who undertakes to pay money or perform in the event that the principal fails to do so.

Time is of the Essence Clause - The Time is of the Essence Clause in a contract is one which emphasizes that the time of performance is so crucial that a breach of the clause may operate to discharge the entire agreement.

Unconscionable - Unconscionable refers to the condition of a contract which is so one-sided and detrimental to the interest of one of the parties that it operates to render the contract unenforceable.

Uniform Commercial Code (UCC) - The UCC is a code of laws governing commercial transactions which was designed to bring uniformity to the laws of the various states.

Unilateral Contract - A unilateral contract is a contract whereby one party makes a promise to do or refrain from doing something in return for actual performance by the other party.

Usury - Usury refers to an excessive and illegal rate of interest.

Waiver - Waiver refers to an intentional and voluntary surrender of a known right.

BIBLIOGRAPHY

Black's Law Dictionary, Fifth Edition. St. Paul, MN: West Publishing Company, 1979.

Burnham, Scott J. *Drafting Contracts, Second Edition.* Charlottesville, VA: The Michie Company, 1993.

Gifis, Steven H. *Barron's Law Dictionary, Second Edition.* Woodbury, NY: Barron's Educational Series, Inc., 1984.

Lawyer's Desk Book, Eighth Edition. Englewood Cliffs, NJ: Institute for Business Planning, Inc., 1985.

Milko, George, Ostberg, Kay and Meehan Rudy, Theresa *Everyday Contracts, Protecting Your Rights: A Step-By-Step Guide.* New York, NY: Random House, 1991.

Neubert, Christopher and Withiam, Jr., Jack *How to Handle Your Own Contracts.* New York, NY: Sterling Publishing Co., Inc., 1991.

Trachtman, Michael G. *What Every Executive Better Know About the Law.* New York, NY: Simon and Schuster, 1987.

White, James J. and Summers, Robert S. *Uniform Commercial Code, Second Edition.* St. Paul, MN: West Publishing Company, 1980.